# HIGH-IMPACT RESOURCES FOR PEAK PERFORMERS

The Single Seat Mindset Insider Circle is designed specifically for peak performers that desire cutting-edge ideas from some of the world's most elite fighter pilots. I would like to extend a personal invitation for you to be a part of our powerful community.

You can get direct access to all of our life changing resources... most of which are no cost to you! Additionally, you can contact me directly to ask your questions that deserve a unique perspective unlike anything found anywhere else in the world— a fighter pilot's perspective.

If you are a peak performer with a "Let's get it done; don't hold me back" attitude and want immediate results, get access now at:

**SingleSeatMindset.com/insider-circle**

Put your talents to good use, and accelerate past all the slow people holding you back from your ambitious goals.

# WHAT OTHERS ARE SAYING:

*"Ever since I've joined the Single Seat Mindset Insider Circle, I've been able to understand what it takes to be successful in every aspect of life."*

—**Jonathan Lightfoot**
**Engineer & Fighter Pilot**

*"Single Seat Mindset is a breath of fresh air amidst the stress of flight training. It reminds me that I'm not alone in my struggles, helps me set realistic goals for myself, and encourages me to keep striving for excellence rather than just meeting the bar."*

—**Carlyann Dean**
**Fighter Pilot**

*"The tenacity and hard-earned truths won by those aviators found within these pages is transferable to anyone who chooses to apply similar actions or mindsets to their own problem set."*

—**Dr. John Gassaway**
**Clinical Aviation Psychologist**

# SINGLE SEAT
# WISDOM

*Practical and Valuable Life Advice*
*From America's Fighter Pilots*

COMPILED BY

DOMINIC "SLICE" TEICH

Print ISBN: 978-1-7351129-2-3
eBook ISBN: 978-1-7351129-8-5

Original cover artwork by Neil Hipkiss, used with permission from Jeffrey Cohen.

Published by Single Seat Mindset, LLC.
082922

## DISCLAIMER

Views expressed in these books are the authors and may not reflect those of the Department of Defense or the United States Military services. Appearance of US DoD visual information does not imply or constitute DoD endorsement.

*Single Seat Wisdom* is dedicated to the Anna Schindler Foundation and all the children in the world that are riddled with cancerous malignancies.

All of you fierce warriors are fighting a battle that is far scarier than anything I have ever done.

You champions give us a strong reminder of how much we have to be thankful for every day and provide us with inspiration that is unmatched.

God bless you on your journey.

**AnnaSchindlerFoundation.org**

## ALSO BY DOMINIC "SLICE" TEICH

*Single Seat Wisdom – Volume 2*

*Single Seat Investor*

*Single Seat Gratitude*

*Single Seat Scratchpad*

*Single Seat Coloring*

**Available at:**

SingleSeatMindset.com/books

# CONTENTS

## PART 3–THE PATH FORWARD

## PART 4–APPENDIX

PART 1

WELCOME

*"You start with a bag full of luck and an empty bag of experience. The trick is to fill the bag of experience before you empty the bag of luck."*

**–Anonymous**

# ACKNOWLEDGEMENT

To Joe and Polly Schindler. Your drive to help families with children riddled with cancer has influenced me in ways I never imagined. Your journey that started when your daughter Anna was diagnosed with hepatoblastoma in 2010 has influenced and shaped the lives of so many, even with the loss of your baby girl, Anna.

Thank you for being a positive influence in my life. We named our baby girl Anna so that her memory can carry on with the Anna Schindler Foundation. All the proceeds from any of our books go directly to your foundation to help families that are going through what you have already painfully endured. God bless your drive and determination to make the world a better place. It has inspired me to trust that God has a bigger plan for everyone; including me! Learn more at: AnnaSchindlerFoundation.org.

*"Good judgment comes from experience. Unfortunately, the experience usually comes from bad judgment."*

**–Anonymous**

# THANK YOU TO OUR DONORS

Without selfless giving, monetary help, and precious time, Single Seat Mindset would not work! To those of you that gave your time and money to make this happen, thank you.

- Drew & Katie Taylor
- Joe & Valerie Goldsworthy
- Mark & Becky Cretella
- Adam & Ashley Luber
- Bradley & Jenny Sullivan
- Kevin & Katie McKernan
- Gregory Kreuder
- Dan & Diana Fletcher
- Patrick & Kirsty Wherry

- Kris & Tiffany Holstege
- Mark Allen
- Bryson & Melissa Byrd
- Monessa & Greg Balzhiser
- Doug & Jenny Slocum
- Chris & Ashley Marslender
- Jeff & Katherine Cohen
- Trena & Ryan Savageau
- Jessa & Chris Charron
- Melissa & Michael May
- Dominic & Danielle Teich
- Isla, Max, Anna & Killian Teich
- Ed Rush
- Robert Coe
- Dan Cartin
- William P. Anton
- Thomas Mueller
- Steven Vallenari
- Michael & Anjulie Broderick
- Michael Terrigino
- Brian & Kathryn Steele
- Joe & Polly Schindler

- Katie, JJ, Maggie, Anna, Gus, Nate, Blake, & Abbie Schindler
- Joe Del Bagno
- Stephen Del Bagno
- Kirk Donathan
- Mike & Becky Capuzzi
- Scott & Christina MacIntyre
- Aaron & Terri Jelinek
- Dr. John Gassaway
- Mike & Mindy Weinstein
- Ryan Gerdes
- Eric Ford
- Tim & Michele Teich
- Phil & Tamra Pecora
- Nolan Sweeney
- Lynn Balzhiser
- Jeannette Crowder

*To get wisdom is better than gold; to get understanding is to be chosen rather than silver.*

**—Proverbs 16:16 (RSV)**

# FOREWORD

*"A great book should leave you with many experiences, and slightly exhausted at the end. You live several lives while reading."*
**—William Styron, Author**

I n my opinion, the book you are reading at this very moment is *a great book*, even though it's not authored by a famous writer, published by some big name publisher, or on some well-known person's "must-read list."

This book is great because the experiences, insights and challenges contained herein will change readers' lives.

Dom "Slice" Teich has done an admirable job of curating a respected group of his fighter pilot peers and getting them to share some of their most profound and inspiring *wisdom*.

Before I get too much further, I have a confession of sorts to make. I am not (was not) a fighter pilot.

*So, why would Dom ask someone, who has never piloted a single seat jet (let alone fly in one), to write the Foreword of a book filled with military pilots and their profound stories?*

To answer that, I need to tell you a little bit about myself. Over the past 24 years since I started my marketing consulting and publishing company, I have had the good fortune to work with thousands of business owners and entrepreneurs from around the world. Throughout these two+ decades, I have encountered a handful of individuals who truly impressed me and inspired me.

*Dom Teich is one of those individuals.*

I first started working with Dom in March 2020. Dom contacted me and was interested in working together to publish a book about his apartment real estate investing business. Immediately after our first call, I realized Dom had that special "It" Factor.

His motivation, work ethic and zeal for constant growth resulted in his first book, *Single Seat Investor,* being published in less than three months. Since then, Dom has worked with me to publish two other books, *Single Seat Gratitude* and *Single Seat Scratchpad*, but none are as profound and important as the book you are now reading.

The idea for *Single Seat Wisdom* came to us in September 2020, and unlike his previous books, this one would require an extraordinary amount of work, project management and motivation. Honestly, there were times I did not think Dom would get it done.

Fortunately, I was wrong.

*Single Seat Wisdom* is one of those special books that truly has the power to transform lives. As I read through the draft manuscripts Dom provided along the way, I felt challenged, inspired, energized, hopeful and even sad at times. More importantly, I felt motivated to up my game because of the stories you are about to read.

In my opinion, one characteristic of a powerful book is its ability to ignite actionable ideas. I believe *Single Seat Wisdom* is going to be THE fuse that ignites the flame of desire for an entire group of future fighter pilots and military officers. But this book is going to do so much more beyond filling our armed forces with quality individuals. *Single Seat Wisdom* will also be a spark for future physicians, entrepreneurs, authors and leaders of all types.

It's that great of a book.

So, buckle in. Check 6. (Thanks Dom!) And get ready for an unforgettable ride!

**–Mike Capuzzi**
MikeCapuzzi.com

*"The engine is the heart of an airplane,
but the pilot is its soul."*

**–Walter Alexander Raleigh**

# PREFACE

This book was written by fantastic human beings that have defied death on many occasions and who challenge the physical and mental complexities of this world.

You guessed it; they are ALL fighter pilots and people that I hold in the highest regard. Their life lessons and perspectives are unique due to the fact that they have traveled the world, fought in combat, stood in harm's way to defend America and even killed the enemy to keep you and I safe. They are defenders of freedom and want to guide you on the road less traveled with their powerful life lessons so that you can apply them to your life and increase your chances of success.

Their wisdom is contained in this book.

You won't find a book published like this one anywhere else. It's one of a kind!

These golden nuggets of wisdom will transform how you perceive the world and your place in it.

Each experience is unique, and each provides helpful advice, guidance, and information on what you could do to reframe the way that you look at life.

By the end of this book, you will realize that you can be more, achieve more, and ultimately be a success. You don't have to take my word for it though. While preparing this book for publication, I was surprised to find answers to many of my own trials and life issues. You can too.

## If You Really Like This Book – Please Consider Giving It Away

Single Seat Mindset LLC is a for-profit business that gives all NET profits to charity. This book was written to help others with short stories and a different life perspective. 100% of the monetary proceeds support the Anna Schindler Foundation—a childhood cancer non-profit. Additionally, our resources impact the lives of readers just like you!

I invite you to reach out to me if you would like more copies that you can give away as gifts. ALL profits from this book continue to support families that are burdened with expensive hospital bills.

If you would like to purchase these books in bulk and you don't need them immediately (coaches, sports teams, schools, business teams), please contact me for affordable pricing, and I will throw in FREE shipping; it's much cheaper than buying them on Amazon, but it will take slightly longer to receive them in the mail.

*What's the catch?*

There isn't one. Single Seat Mindset is a collection of fighter pilots that want to help you. They want to be there for you in the form of story and digital content even if you don't live in their neck of the woods. Distribution of these books is easier for everyone if we continue to share them and get the message out.

Our goal is to guide you and help charity.

Please help us by sharing—don't let this book sit on a shelf and collect dust. Use it as a reference guide to provide a different perspective on events, trials, and tribulations that you have in your daily life.

**SingleSeatMindset.com**

*Desire to succeed.*
*Challenge yourself.*
*Be the best.*

**—Dominic "Slice" Teich**
Founder—Single Seat Mindset

*"A fighter pilot's ability to juggle information, sustain flight, master and overcome illusions, and rely on their wits and intuition builds a formidable self-reliance.*

*It is with this understanding of what a single seater is that I implore you to head the messages, advice, and perceptions held within these pages. This book holds interesting insights and knowledge that will be valuable to you. The author is a professional fighter pilot, with knowledge beyond simply aviation."*

**—Dr. John Gassaway**
**Clinical Psychologist**

# WHO SHOULD READ
# SINGLE SEAT WISDOM?

The fact that you are holding this book in your hand and reading it is no accident; now is the time. If you are taking the time to read these words now, I'm confident that you are searching for something, thinking of how you can make a difference, and putting in the *effort* to get there.

I'd also bet that you don't think that life is just handed to you and there are no long-term lucky people; but I'd like to disagree. The people you see and want to emulate have put themselves in situations, tackled the difficult things in life, put in their study and diligent work, and prepared for their lucky break. What you are doing right now is the same thing: preparing yourself so when the time is right, you are ready and you can be successful too based on your past efforts.

*Luck* is a combination of *timing* plus hyper-focused *effort*.

In America, you can put your mind to something and make it happen. Due to technology, even physical abnormalities aren't holding many back from achieving their dreams. I'm not implying that everyone is cut out to be a fighter pilot, astronaut, or doctor, but rather stating that due to this amazing country we live in, you can BE something much bigger here than you could be elsewhere in the world.

What you'll find is that your mindset drives decisions in your life that will differentiate you from other people that don't take the time to improve. Leverage the unique mindset of single seat jet fighter pilots and their unique training and experiences in the third dimension.

## Who This Book Is For:

- Active or Aspiring Pilots.
- Parents and Children.
- Students and Athletes.
- Business Owners & Entrepreneurs.
- A gift for someone that has potential.
- Coaches and Sports Teams.
- Anyone looking for a unique viewpoint.

## Who This Books Is Not For:

- Individuals that lack initiative.
- Lazy people.
- People that think the world is unfair.
- Someone that wants a handout.
- Dreamers that don't take action.

Put in the **effort** now so that when the **time** is right, you'll get your **lucky** break.

*"Every takeoff is optional.
Every landing is mandatory."*

**—Anonymous**

# MY PROMISE TO YOU

Speaking about trouble achieving success, if you're struggling and only moderately successful, frustration can set in. I fought back for years and felt like the world was pushing me around. I felt like my talents could be put to a better use. But I turned into a workaholic, and many times, it wasn't fun. Struggling to get it done and attack the newest challenge, I would get stuck in a routine that caused burnout. Through this process, I learned a few tricks.

When the world pushed me, I pushed back. My impatience with the slow people around me came off the wrong way, and it hindered a lot of the forward progress that I could have made due to a poor mindset. Feeling stuck, I took matters into my own hands and considered struggle a necessary part of the process. What I didn't know at the time was that struggling for too long can leave you feeling aggravated and can lead to mental blocks that make you think that your current problems will subsist forever and you won't be successful. This can negatively impact your chances of success. At the time, I didn't realize that the journey is the fun part.

*What would it look like for you to achieve your goals? Would you know that success can come no matter what?*

Do you want to:

- *BE a bigger version of yourself?*
- *BE the best in your category?*
- *Come and go as you please?*
- *Help others more effectively?*
- *Build greater returns on investments?*
- *Earn financial independence?*
- *Earn extra income?*
- *Achieve more free time to do the things that are important to you?*

You may think you are struggling because you don't know your life's purpose. So, imagine my surprise when I found out you don't have to know the end state to take inspired action. In fact, the best way to find your purpose is to go out and try bold, new things—a **Single Seat Mindset**.

Experts will tell you that fear of failure can completely derail your chances of success, and they are correct. *So, why not flip the fear around and use it as motivation to achieve your biggest goals?* Take the lie and make it the truth. I don't fear failure. I embrace it and consider it a necessary step in the process to becoming something more.

Thanks to what all the authors of this book are sharing with you today, people everywhere are now creating success generating habits that last a lifetime. Consider this book a jumpstart to eliminate procrastination for good and to attack your inner critic because it may be the source of your problems!

If you are looking to experience success on autopilot and generate a positive **Single Seat Mindset** that you can apply to all aspects of your daily life, you'll find it here in the pages of this book. Others that have applied these lessons in wisdom have added purpose to everything they do.

*Will you?*

*"To accomplish great things, we must not only act but also dream, not only plan but also believe."*

**–Anatole France**

# INTRODUCTION

**M**ore than ever in American history, we are seeing an unprecedented and damaging worldview that goes a little bit like this: *"I am entitled to *insert entitlement* because of *insert excuse here*."*

People aren't willing to work towards worthwhile goals because they are too scared that it will be uncomfortable and that they might fail. You can easily outshine, excel, and dominate your sphere of influence if you have a plan.

## Why This Is Important Now!

Lazy people aren't willing to put the time and effort into their dreams and will be stuck behind you, complaining about life. If you simply show up, you will be ahead of others. If you show up prepared, you will set yourself up to reap the rewards of luck that is a byproduct of timing and hyperfocused effort.

You may catch a lucky break and get a handout now and again, but that view of the world doesn't have any long-term benefits. If you can't duplicate past success, then you only achieved a moderate gain that might not help you in the long-term.

Something you may have tried in the past that let you down was adding more projects to a to-do list, and that probably burned you out because the bigger your to-do list got, the more stress and overload it created.

A much better approach is to first focus on eliminating what you don't need to get done, and begin saying "no" to tasks that aren't a priority. If it's not THE priority, don't do it. Have a plan.

If you have a plan, when the time is right, you will be ready.

## Invitation to Contact Me

The authors of this book are a lot like you; however, they have had some unique experiences. These led to insights that you'll find extremely helpful.

Meet the world's largest group of fighter pilots sharing their wisdom in print, audio, and digital formats.

When it comes to success, I believe you need to be choosy.

Finally, there is a radically different approach to life you can trust.

In the world of success, Single Seat Mindset will change everything. Join the Single Seat Mindset Insider Circle today at:

**SingleSeatMindset.com/insider-circle**

PART 2

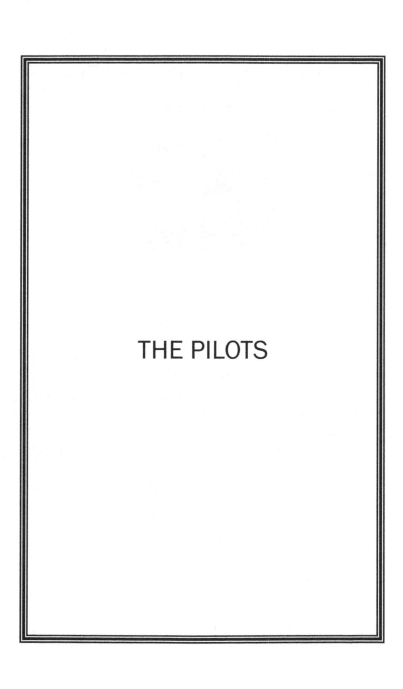

# THE PILOTS

# DREW "APOLLO" TAYLOR

"Apollo" is a husband, father, and instructor pilot in the F-16 fighter jet. He is passionate about helping people like you reach new heights through faith, leadership, and relationships. From teaching skydiving to leading high-stress combat operations, he strives to take the millions of dollars the military has invested in him to help develop others to reach their highest potential. When Apollo and his wife, Katie, are not rock climbing, skiing, or living life to the fullest with their kids, they are busy as the founders of *To The Heights Ministry* and recording videos on Catholic-Link.org (YouTube channel) to try to help as many people as possible.

*"Be amazed at the heights to which you are called."*
**—Saint Pope John Paul II**

To learn more about how Drew and Katie can help you with your faith journey, relationships, or attainting your God-given purpose in life, please visit them at: ToTheHeightsMinistry.com.

# CHAPTER #1

# CROSS-CHECK

Before officers go to pilot training in the United States Air Force, they complete a program designed to evaluate whether they have what it takes to graduate: Initial Flight Screening. This program delivers information like a firehose, fast and violent, especially for those with little to no flying experience. The mental crucible is a significant first step in their quest to become Air Force pilots.

On my fifth flight in the program, I took to the skies on a crisp, windy Colorado day with my instructor pilot in the DA-20 Katana aircraft. As we were accomplishing a practice landing, my instructor pulled back the throttle simulating my engine had failed. My job as the student was to safely land the airplane, which essentially had just been turned into a glider. As I maneuvered back to the runway, task saturated but determined to control the tiny aircraft being tossed around like a paper plane, it became evident that I wasn't going to make the approach, so I decided to go around and try again. Unfortunately, I didn't realize that I had lost track of how close I was to the ground, and by the time I made this decision, it was too late.

I rapidly advanced the power, and in a split second, a crosswind picked up our plane and ripped our left wing through the runway's asphalt like a cheese grater. The collision caused the aircraft to cartwheel wing-over-wing off the side of the runway.

The plane did three complete flips, which broke the wings, smashed the propeller, collapsed the landing gear, snapped the tail, and shattered the canopy. But our guardian angels must have been watching over us that day because, miraculously, we landed right-side-up without a scratch.

I'll never forget the look on my instructor's face when he turned to me and said in a low, disappointed voice, *"We should egress now."*

This was not the way I envisioned starting my Air Force career and my dream to become a fighter pilot. After an investigation, the Air Force reluctantly re-instated me, and I made it through the program. I continued to Undergraduate Pilot Training, and with an immense amount of grit, I graduated pilot training the following year at the top of my class and assigned to fly the F-16 fighter jet. But even after achieving my goal, instead of smooth sailing, life was just as turbulent as that day I crashed. If I excelled in my job, my marriage or family suffered; I struggled to find the correct definition that would lead to success. My pain led me towards a desire to have a plan and process for my life that I could duplicate.

One of the best tools I learned in the process of becoming a fighter pilot is called a "*cross-check*." It's a scan through the cockpit to gather information, analyze situations, and make decisions that lead to success during the mission. Developing a cross-check fills gaps and prioritizes what is important in the current moment.

The word prioritize comes from the Latin word, *priōritās*, meaning first in time, importance, or rank. The key here is there can only be one priority. Stephen Covey said, "*The main thing is to keep the main thing the main thing.*"

Because of their nature, peak performers can often have 36 different priorities; this leads to overload, failure, and confusion when the correct processes aren't in place. *So, how do high achievers devote time effectively to exclusively concentrate on only the essential things in life that matter?*

While flying, the answer is to develop a cross-check, where you hyperfocus only on the essential gage, sensor, or surroundings to correctly fly the jet, make radio calls, shoot missiles, and drop bombs. It's knowing precisely what to look at exactly when you need it, a checklist of importance where your focus is directed towards the most critical thing at the right time and nothing else. It is this technique that has created the greatest fighter pilots in history.

In addition to building a cross-check, modern fighter jets have programmable warning systems to alert the pilot when something is wrong. These systems are critical to cross-check. When flying at the speed of sound with only one engine, it's crucial to know if your engine is on fire! In the F-16 fighter jet, I now set altitude warnings to know when I am too close to the ground to avoid crashing another airplane.

However, in my quest to become a successful fighter pilot, it still seemed like my life was on the verge of becoming a colossal mishap. I remember looking at the older pilots and wondering how they did it all. It wasn't until a meeting with my commander one day that I figured out the answer.

The day after becoming an instructor pilot in the F-16, he sat me down and asked me questions about how I planned to handle all of my new responsibilities at work while still keeping the rest of my life in check. There was a long pause before I quietly admitted, *"I don't know, sir. I guess it'll just take more grit, and I'll have to work harder."* He smiled and explained that the most successful fighter pilots use a cross-check not just for flying but also for the important aspects of their lives. They figure out what they need to prioritize and are relentless in their focus. Whether it is faith, marriage, family, work, service to their country and community, or health and fitness, they are disciplined in cross-checking success indicators and setting up warning lights to alert them before disaster strikes.

That conversation, along with my near-death experience of crashing a plane, helped clarify that there comes a point in your life where more grit isn't the answer. What I needed to consider was setting my proper priority for the infinite game. Often, people's biggest regret on their deathbed is not having devoted enough focus to their relationships.

*So how are your relationships with God, your family, and your loved ones?*

*Who will still be there when you retire, and what do you want them to say about you when you die?*

*What would you change in your life if you lived with your perspective focused on eternity?*

Take your family, for example. Family is like a fuel tank in a fighter jet. F-16 pilots meticulously check their gas because fuel runs out within minutes if the throttle is left in afterburner! Many pilots are fueled by their families but often poorly prioritize their cross-check and flame out at home because they leave the throttle in afterburner in their professional lives and forget to leave some gas in the tank to power the machine at home. There are times when after-burner is required in short spurts in life, but always set a fuel warning for your family, or you will cause them to flame out!

I've applied this lesson to everything from dropping bombs in combat to changing diapers. In 2019, I was selected to go to Weapons School, the Air Force's equivalent of TOPGUN (U.S. Navy). Before I left, I cross-checked my family and decided that it would be better to take them with me for six months than to leave them behind (something very few fighter pilots choose to do). This was my way of prioritizing them as much as I could at the time. I figured even one dinner a week, Saturday at the park with the kids, and going to church with them on Sunday was better than not seeing them for half a year.

It turned out to be one of the best decisions I have ever made.

Halfway through Weapons School, I underwent neck surgery, and because I kept my family in my cross-check, they got to spend that time with me versus being stuck at my previous base in another country. Their encouragement due to a good cross-check was invaluable, and I credit my ability to return to Weapons School and graduate in the next class to their support.

I've learned we are all one violent gust of wind away from crashing in life. Having a cross-check has made me a better husband, father, and better version of myself. It's a huge reason why my wife and I started *To The Heights Ministry*. We felt driven to help people reach new heights in their faith by living life to the fullest, building supportive communities, and creating family cultures with on-fire marriages. We hope that the lessons we've learned will help you do the same.

---

### Apollo's Wisdom:

The small and important decisions you make every day directly influence the outcome of your life and those around you. Some choices could lead you to crash and burn. However, if you prioritize correctly, set up your warning systems, and develop a disciplined cross-check, you will reach new heights in your life!

---

# JOE "SLAP" GOLDSWORTHY

Since 2001, "Slap" has been a USAF Fighter Pilot. He started flying at age 11 and has 4,000+ hours among F-35, A-10, AMX (Italian), T-38, and many civilian aircraft. His other passion is farming, and today he splits his time between flying jets and driving tractors on his farm near Spokane, Washington. In his spare time, he likes spending time with his kids. He believes his #1 priority in life is being a great dad and sharing life lessons and experience with them, both good and bad.

*"If it's worth doing,
it's worth overdoing."*

**–Ayn Rand**

Email Slap at A10SLAP@yahoo.com.

# CHAPTER #2

# ATTITUDE & ENTITLEMENT

My pilot training class patch had a saying inscribed *"Attitude is Everything."* If there is one key factor to my successes and failures in life, I can generally trace it back to the problem I faced and the attitude to which I approached it.

I grew up on a rural wheat farm where working at a young age was a fact of life. It wasn't always enjoyable, but I learned some of the most important life lessons working with seemingly ancient relatives who had grown up on that same farm during a different era.

My great-uncle and my grandfather were in their late 60's at the time and never short on stories about work ethic or pointing out my generation's lack thereof; in my defense, I was only 10.

Often with a bit of sarcastic ridicule towards my generation, they thought kids my age had an entitled attitude, that we felt deserving of things we had not yet earned and that we, in essence, were a bit lazy.

This ridicule would be followed up with a pointed story about those unwilling to put in the effort going hungry during the great depression or a childhood story about being my age and driving teams of horses around the same fields that I luckily drove a tractor through or how I took a bus to school while they walked. They would later own up to some embellishment, but the theme was always there: how hard they worked growing up, how nothing was given to them, how they never expected anything and how they were better off for it.

I brushed this off as a couple of old farmers poking fun at me at the time, but as I grew older, I realized they cared about my attitude towards life and work and had been sharing specific lessons with me. The majority of these pointed at one specific theme:

*I was entitled to nothing that I didn't earn.*

As I got older, I learned more about the two old guys doling out life advice and how they would shape my future.

My grandfather had been a World War II pilot shot down during a bombing raid over Tokyo. He spent many months in a Japanese prison camp barely surviving the war, a feat he attributed to his attitude and outlook. He later flew in the Korean War and became a 2-star general.

His older brother, my great-uncle, had been a pilot and 3-star general donning the cover of magazines, then after the military, living a comfortable life as a well-paid consultant.

Both had worked from a life of being poor farm kids during the Great Depression to becoming pilots and military officers. Yet here they were, in their retirement years working as hard as ever on the farm and sharing their most important life lessons with me, and I didn't even know it.

They were my childhood heroes, and I was determined to follow in their footsteps as military officers and pilots to make them proud.

My first memorable life lesson on attitude and entitlement that still affects me was sports related.

I played eight-man (yes, that's "8") football in my rural high school, and to a small town, it was a very big deal. During my junior year, a new kid joined the team mid-season, and I gave little thought to him until he took my starting position. My grandfather had made a trip to see me play one Friday, but that night I was on the bench. I was embarrassed and ashamed, but the life lesson was well deserved. I had gotten lazy and comfortable...felt entitled to my spot, and in doing so, I was outworked by someone who wanted it more. I can still remember seeing my grandfather there, the letdown I felt and how much I hated that feeling. I vowed I wouldn't be on the bench long. I worked like I had been taught and earned my position back. It's a seemingly small event that still affects me today as I remember the cause, the feeling which I never wanted to repeat, and the fix.

*I was entitled to nothing I didn't earn.*

I would later attend the same college that both my grandfather and great-uncle attended. Their lessons were always in the back of my mind as I worked to become a pilot and achieve my goal of flying fighter jets. A lot of people I knew wanted what I did, but I knew that the ones that would make it happen were the ones willing to work the hardest and sacrifice to get there.

Another standout work ethic lesson was when I went to pilot training. I showed up having a considerable amount of civilian flying time that I had hoped would give me an edge. At first it did, and I cruised through the basic phases with ease until one day I didn't. At one point, I was sitting on flight busts in a row while others had caught up. Just like with the football lesson I learned, the cause was the same. I had gotten complacent with my performance and a bit lazy because I had done well at first, and felt entitled to a fighter slot. I was being outworked, and it was showing.

Luckily, I realized this problem quickly, the result of building on previous experience, all tracing back to those lessons on the farm years before.

*I was entitled to nothing that I didn't earn.*

I earned my fighter, and my grandfather attended my graduation proudly. Over the next 20 years, I went on to fly thousands of hours in multiple aircraft. I slipped up at times, growing content with my performance but was swiftly brought back to earth by failure and facing the reality that success in life was never going to be handed to me and that I'd always have to work for it.

This brings me to today, older as my career flying fighters winds down, I decided to run that small farm I grew up on. I visit it often, with fond memories of the lessons I learned there from people who had learned those same lessons decades earlier about approaching hard work with a good attitude. The farm barely pays for itself, requires constant upkeep and work, and I'm often asked, *"Why do you do it?"*

The answer is simple.

I have two kids now that come to the farm with me, and both want to be military pilots. While we do various jobs, I tell them my tales about growing up there and joke with them about their generation's entitled attitude and work ethic. My son starts to complain about how much he's working and how little he's being paid, and I stop him mid-sentence, excitedly wanting to share the lesson that has benefitted me the most in life, calmly but sternly, I say, *"You are not entitled to anything you don't earn."*

By the look on his face, the words are not appreciated. At least not yet.

---

**Slap's Wisdom:**

You are not entitled to anything you don't earn.

---

*"Enjoy the little things, for one day you may look back and realize they were the big things."*

**−Robert Brault**

# MARK "CREATURE" CRETELLA

"Creature" flew F-16s in the United States Air Force and retired in 2021 after a 20-year career. He and his wife, Becky, live in Phoenix with their four children. Creature is currently a military contractor with the goal of flying for an airline, but who knows? The Cretella family looks forward to whatever the future holds.

*"When you come to a fork in the road, take it."*

**–Yogi Berra**

Email Creature at cretella@hotmail.com.

# CHAPTER 3

# ACCEPTANCE

Most people do not like to use the word "surrender." It often connotes failure. However, it also means "to give oneself over to something." If you have ever been to the ocean, you have probably heard the advice that you should not fight against a rip current. You will become exhausted and possibly drown. You should let the current pull you out to sea, then swim away from the rip in order to safely make it back to shore. This form of surrender can help one to accept and make the most of life's circumstances.

One of the first times I faced what I thought was a major setback in life was when I received my first assignment out of pilot training in the Air Force. It was an exciting time in my life. I was going to get my wings, get married, and then get to fly a fighter. Except on assignment night, after a year of dreaming about getting to be an F-15 Eagle pilot, I found out I was actually going to stay at my current base and teach students the basics of flying.

I was pretty upset for a couple of weeks. I really thought I deserved a chance to fly an F-15. I could not imagine all of my friends getting to fly combat mission in A-10s, F-16s, and F-15s while I was stuck for three years teaching students how to take off and land. However, I remember a day, just a couple of weeks after graduating, when I was hiking with my soon-to-be wife, Becky. It was a beautiful day, and we had an awesome view looking down over the farms and prairies that I would soon be instructing over, and I realized I had an opportunity. I would get to have a great impact on future Air Force pilots. And a T-37 instructor's life is not nearly as busy as a fighter pilot's life, which worked out well, as Becky and I were married right after I graduated.

During this assignment, while talking to pilots who had flown various fighters, I decided that I really didn't want to fly the Eagle after all. I wanted to fly the Viper! Life's detour led me to do what I was really meant to do, which was to fly the multi-role F-16. I loved it. I ultimately got to teach in the F-16 schoolhouse, and my years in the T-37 helped me be a better instructor for the many F-16 students I taught. I got the chance early in life to see that sometimes you just have to go with the flow of life.

Another "setback" I experienced was when I was not selected for promotion to Lieutenant Colonel. I was on an 18-month assignment, separated from my family, as an exchange pilot in Jordan when I got the news. I was bummed, as I saw once again a lot of my peers moving along in their career progression while I now seemed to stagnate.

But I learned from my previous career speed bump and was determined not to dwell on the negative. I was not going to fight the undertow; I was going to flow with a new opportunity. Once again, I found that what I thought I wanted wasn't the best situation for me, my family, or the Air Force. Once I was passed over for rank, I was no longer caught up in the grind for career progression. I was assigned back to Luke Air Force Base, where I was able to focus on instructing pilots upgrading in the F-16. I gave the most value to the Air Force this way, as there was just starting to be a large deficit of fighter pilots. It was also good for my family because we got to stay in Arizona for six years until I retired, which was a huge amount of stability for an active-duty pilot.

My family needed that stability a few years later. I was back home on the East Coast for my mother's funeral when I received a devastating call. Becky and I were waiting for some tests for our daughter, Anna, who had swollen lymph nodes for a couple of months.

The results had come back, and while the doctors weren't certain yet, they had a suspicion that it was serious. My wife asked me to come home immediately. I cannot describe how long a flight is from Boston to Phoenix when you don't know what the future holds for your daughter.

When I arrived at Phoenix Children's Hospital later that night, it was confirmed. My daughter had been diagnosed with leukemia. The next week was a blur, between chemotherapy, scans, labs, and having a port installed. Each day, it was just a mission to figure out what procedures were scheduled and who the doctors and nurses were while also taking care of our other three children.

But this is something we had to accept, and so did Anna. It took her some time. The first month in the hospital she was depressed and bristled at the hospital staff. She just wanted to be home and things to go back to what they were before the diagnosis. But after a month or two, she surrendered to her situation. She began to look forward to seeing her favorite nurses. She liked to stop at the Starbucks in the hospital after chemo to get her favorite drink. For her lumbar punctures, she even turned down anesthetics so that she could get done faster. There was no way to change the diagnosis, but she learned to change how she reacted. After two and a half years, Anna completed her treatment like a true champion of acceptance.

*So, how can you apply this to your life?* Like everything else, you must be conscious of your situation and reaction. Start with the small things, and you will be a little more prepared when a major event happens. I still struggle accepting bad circumstances. It is okay to still feel frustration and impatience; we are not robots and the feelings are natural. We are simply trying to get through those feelings to get moving in the right direction. Rarely does life completely close a door on us without another unexpected opportunity arising in its place. The key is to be ready to move on from your expectations and be ready to surrender to a different, and likely better, outcome.

---

### Creature's Wisdom:

1. Be conscious of your situation and reaction.

2. Start small so you are ready for life's big punches when they happen. Examine your feelings, and try to see the hidden meaning.

3. Manage your expectations so you can surrender to a different path that will likely result in a better outcome.

---

# ADAM "NASTY" LUBER

"Nasty" grew up in Northern California. He went to college in San Diego and commissioned through Air Force ROTC. He went through pilot training at Euro NATO Joint Jet Pilot Training (ENJJPT) and subsequently went on to fly the F-15E Strike Eagle. Additionally, he met his wife while in pilot training.

Nasty went on two combat deployments and was an evaluator pilot during the eight years he flew the F-15E. He and his wife also grew their family during that time and now have two children. In 2017, Nasty transitioned from the F-15E to the F-35A. Outside of flying, Nasty is an entrepreneur, business coach, and investor.

# CHAPTER 4

# FIGHTER PILOT FATHERHOOD

As a fighter pilot, we stress our minds and bodies willingly. We are accustomed to stressful situations and extremely proficient in fighting through stress, fighting through changes, and fighting to win at all costs. This mindset begins before we even strap into our first airplane.

One of the first things we become aware of is the need to take control. Take control of the aircraft, the situation, our emotions, and our fears. This resiliency skill is formed over countless years of practice through exposure to challenging situations. We plan and train for the worst and the most dangerous outcomes. And if we fail, we spend hours and hours understanding why we failed and how we could win the next time. We don't surrender; we don't quit. We adapt, critically think, revise, and live to fight another day.

After seven years of flying, I found myself in the worst-case scenario, and I was woefully unprepared. About 8-10 hours into the situation, I found my surroundings and environment changing at a pace that my mental processing could not keep up with. Aural beeps that were once calming and rhythmic became slow and erratic, and a somewhat sterile environment became chaotic. I played the scenario out in my mind one hundred times prior, but this contingency, I never anticipated. My beautiful wife was in labor, and we were preparing for our firstborn child. We elected to be surprised with the gender of the baby, and we were both extremely anxious to find out if we had a baby boy or girl. Until you go through the process of having a child, it is hard to comprehend the number of consecutive miracles which must take place to have a healthy crying baby breathe its first gasp of air. In our case, we were down to the final minutes of consecutive miracles when the unplanned events began.

Enter my nightmare; alarm bells ringing, doctors and nurses frantically filled the hospital room, and my wife began to panic. I'm frozen with only my eyes tracking each person rushing over to aid. The doctors and nurses are speaking in medical jargon, and my wife and I are caught in an unknown whirlwind. The medical staff immediately start acting without explaining what is happening to us. My wife is placed on 100% oxygen. The doctor ceases the natural birthing process and elects for emergency surgery. As fast as they rushed into the room, they were just as quick to take my wife to the operating room. The frantic hustling in the room was over, the alarm bells ceased, and I was all alone in the room sitting in the same position as when it started. A few minutes later, a nurse explained that my wife had to be put to sleep for the procedure. She also informed me what happened moments ago. The once calming rhythmic beeps which turned slow and erratic were our child's heartbeat. His heartrate continued to slow during her contractions to the point of quitting altogether. The nurse returned to the operating room leaving me alone to weep.

Subconsciously, I began applying the mindset and resiliency that I learned throughout my time flying. I began compartmentalizing different thoughts and different outcomes. *Was the baby okay? Was my wife going to make it? Was I going to be a single parent? If it is a girl, should I name her after her mother?* I had to take control of my situation, my emotions and my mental state just like I had done every time I strapped into a mighty war machine. *How do I take control?* Due to my fighter pilot training, I had grown accustomed to being in control of dangerous situations, but I found myself powerless. All I could do was control my thoughts and my emotions. I could not control the baby's heartbeat. I could not control the surgeon's hands. I could not control my wife's response to the procedure. For the first time, I was powerless and unable to control a situation for my family. There was only one thing that could be done, one thing that I would normally be against—surrender.

I fell to my knees and surrendered to the only one who has control, Almighty God. This was not a difficult decision for me. I grew up in a Catholic family and went to Catholic schools as a kid. It is also not the first time I have surrendered and asked for God's divine intervention. It was the final miracle in a long nine-month process, and time stood still.

About 30 minutes later, the door to the hospital room opened and I was congratulated with a healthy baby boy. My wife also made a full recovery, and it turned out to be a wonderful ending to horrifying situation.

Whether you are religious or not, whether life moves beyond your control, whether you find yourself on your first combat sortie, all humans seek a higher being for comfort and strength. Take a brief moment to remember your why, your purpose, your mission. Relight the fire in your bones, and make a positive move in the direction you want to go. I have learned the following lessons many times over, and I'm sure I will relearn them in the future.

## Nasty's Wisdom:

1. Control what you can control.

- What is in your sphere of control?

- What do you have the ability to do that will positively influence the outcome?

2. Influence what you cannot control.

- The more you educate yourself, the more effective your influence will be.

- The more experiences you find yourself vulnerable in, the more experience-based influence you can have.

3. If you cannot influence or control, then begin learning to further your education.

- We live in the information age.

- Free information is abundant.

- Continue to learn and further a growth mindset.

4. If you find yourself frozen and powerless, surrender control to a higher being, or remember your why, your purpose, your mission.

# BRAD "VAPOR" SULLIVAN

"Vapor" is an accomplished leader, fighter pilot, husband, and father of four who has devoted his life to service: to his faith, family and his country. Lt. Col. Sullivan's story is one of challenge, tragedy and faith. His journey will inspire you to recognize that God has a beautiful plan and purpose for our lives—a plan that is sometimes difficult to see or understand. Sullivan's personal story shows us that ultimately, we can rest in the assurance that God is loving and sovereign.

*"For I know the plans I have for you, declares the Lord, plans to prosper you and not to harm you, plans to give you hope and a future."*
**–Jeremiah 29:11 (NIV)**

Email Vapor at bradsulli@gmail.com.

# CHAPTER #5

# PERSPECTIVE

It was a warm Texas summer night; country music blared from the jukebox. Clear skies and a warm breeze accompanied the peaceful flow of the Frio River. The open-air pavilion was crowded with couples dancing the Texas Two Step. I spotted a pretty young lady standing on the edge of the dance floor, mustered up some courage, and asked if she would like to dance. She obliged.

My story with Sara began.

Sara and I grew up in Houston but attended different schools. The fact that we met at a campground seven hours west of our hometowns but only lived 20 miles apart seemed more than a coincidence. We dated long distance while attending different colleges, but after our freshman year, Sara dumped me.

After college graduation, we reconnected and Sara now agreed that we were meant to be together.

Prior to getting accepted to the Air Force as a pilot, I took Sara back to the dance floor where we met and asked her to be my wife. Once again, she obliged.

During pilot training, Sara and I married and started our travels from Texas to Arizona, Korea, and eventually, Japan. Sara was active in the spouse's group, taught English to local Japanese women, and led exercise classes. Though we missed being close to our families back in Texas, we developed lifelong relationships with other fighter pilots and their families. Somehow, Asia felt like home.

Our assignment in Japan started a life-altering journey when we found a lump in Sara's breast. Prior to our findings, Sara and I had been trying to start a family. Doctors were confident that Sara's situation was benign and that we shouldn't put our lives on hold; I was concerned. During the medical work-up, we found out that Sara was pregnant.

To complicate matters, the Japanese medical facility did not have the expertise or equipment required to diagnose her condition, so we were medically evacuated to Hawaii. Our troubles continued in Hawaii where doctors confirmed the presence of cancer in her breast and lymph nodes. The doctors gave us three options: (1) Terminate the pregnancy, and start treatment immediately. (2) Delay treatment until birth. (3) Tailor treatment slightly, but go forward with surgery and chemotherapy during pregnancy.

We chose option 3.

A whirlwind of life changes ensued in the next few weeks. We gained closure on our assignment in Japan, traveled back to Hawaii for surgery, and eventually settled in Texas to be closer to family.

Chemotherapy treatments began, coupled with a crushing schedule of medical appointments. Sara lost her hair after the second dose of chemo, and we had a head-shaving party. She was the most beautiful bald lady I had ever seen and rocked the bald look most of the time.

Although Sara's pregnancy was complicated, our miracle-baby, Chloe Grace, arrived seven weeks early and in great health. Unfortunately, the week following our release from the hospital, Sara started experiencing significant headaches which resulted in a seizure and subsequent frenzied rush to the hospital. The findings did not point to any specific health issue, which was devastating as Sara rested in a semicomatose state.

Four days after the seizure, Sara's cerebral artery ruptured and compressed her brain, cutting off blood supply. My wife was declared brain dead 14 days after giving birth.

Our family and Sara's medical team circled around as her heart took its final beat—my new reality as a grieving husband and new father unfolded before my eyes.

After the funeral, I embarked on a new chapter. I continued to express gratitude for my daughter, but single parenthood was challenging and demanding. Hours became days. Days became weeks. Weeks became months. Fortunately, my Air Force family stepped in to help in a big way. Fundraisers, meals, and home cleaning enabled my return to work coupled with world-class help from a wife in the fighter squadron who volunteered to be Chloe's nanny.

During our battle with cancer, we started a family blog to keep friends and family informed. As Sara progressed through treatment, the blog spread aggressively to other circles. Chloe received packages from South Africa, Australia, Europe, and Asia. I was amazed at the expansive spread and number of lives that were impacted by the life of Sara Sullivan, even though she was no longer with us.

A widow told me during my journey, *"It's okay to go into the pit of despair, but you must immediately begin the climb out. You cannot stay there."* That statement was life-changing for me. My blog allowed thoughts to flow to paper for other's encouragement in troubling times, and I made conscious efforts to "choose JOY!" Although life was challenging at every turn, I always tried to find something to be thankful for. My daughter reminded me every day that Sara and I made the right decision.

Through multiple random connections, I became a pen pal with a widow named Jenny. Jenny's husband lost the battle against bone cancer leaving behind two young children entrusted to her care. We both had something in common: single parenthood and loss of a spouse to cancer. It didn't take long for us to fall in love, get married, and become a family of five. The next few years included a deployment, another child, a three-year assignment to Germany to fly F-16s, and finally a homecoming to the USA. Upon our return, I adopted Jenny's two children (Zeke and Kaelyn), and Jenny adopted Chloe; paperwork now matched what we felt in our hearts.

Comparing who I am today with who I was before Sara's cancer diagnosis, it's hard to believe the personal growth and understanding of life that has developed. Life transforms amidst tragic circumstances. Grief comes in all shapes and sizes as it's a universal feeling all people experience. How you process grief determines who you become.

For a more detailed read through of this journey, visit BandSSullivan.blogspot.com.

---

**Vapor's Wisdom:**

1. You cannot always control what happens to you, but you must be responsible and accountable for your actions.

2. You don't realize your full potential until you are face-to-face with significant trials.

3. It's okay and healthy to ask for help. Don't let your pride stand in the way.

4. When times are tough, it's easy to focus on problems. No matter how bad the situation, there are others going through tougher times than you. If you look hard enough, there are always things to be thankful for. It's all about PERSPECTIVE.

---

*"There are only two ways to live your life. One is as though nothing is a miracle. The other is as though everything is a miracle."*

**—Albert Einstein**

# KEVIN "POPEYE" MCKERNAN

"Popeye" began his time as a fighter pilot in the F-16 "Viper" where he amassed 1100 hours of flight time, including 420 hours in combat. He then transitioned to the F-35 Lightning II, which he currently flies. He lives in Phoenix, AZ, with his stunningly gorgeous wife, Katie, and their three amazing children.

*"Even though I walk through the valley of the shadow of death,*
*I fear no evil, for thou art with me."*

**–Psalm 23-4 (NASB)**

# CHAPTER 6

# MATURITY AS A MATTER OF CHOICE

O ver the radio, the words crackled, *"Viper 61, JAG 22, good effects, building destroyed, six enemy K.I.A. Mission successful."*

The first time I heard those words, circling over Afghanistan at 20,000 feet, I was too busy to fully process what they meant or what I had just done. My mental task load on a combat sortie was simply too high to allow for existential thoughts. Your thoughts focus on executing the job, accomplishing the mission, and going home.

After landing my F-16, it was a different story. You download the data from the airplane, enabling you to rewatch the mission, looking for errors. Analyzing your mission works to improve your and your fellow pilots' skills and provides valuable information to higher headquarters. Post flight, you get to watch high-definition footage from the jet's infrared targeting sensor of your bombs and rockets exploding as you verify your decision making and ensure you hit the correct target.

The first time I truly understood the reality of taking a human life, I was in an office chair, coffee cup in hand as the results of my choices were shown in high definition. Only one week into my six-month deployment, I knew that I had to figure out how to deal with this reality if I was going to be able to do my job effectively long-term; something I signed up for but didn't realize the gravity of until it became my reality.

I had two options. I could avoid the introspection, treat the entire situation like a video game and leave the truth of what I did unacknowledged in my own mind. Alternatively, I could admit that my choices and actions had consequences that affected the lives of numerous people. I had to accept that those consequences gave me a vast amount of personal responsibility to ensure I was making the best possible decisions.

Before leaving for my first deployment, I certainly looked like a mature adult on paper. I was a college graduate, had been married for three years and was the proud father of a beautiful baby girl. Professionally, I was a captain in the United States Air Force, had completed pilot training and was a fighter pilot flying F-16s out of Aviano Air Base in northern Italy.

However, I had a childish mindset in how I processed and handled the events of my own life. I did not understand this at the time, but none of my "adult' accomplishments had anything to do with adulthood or maturity. I did not consider myself immature. *How could I?* I had done so much, accomplished so much. I was a 28-year-old father, husband, and fighter pilot. *What else did I need to do?*

What I failed to understand at the time is that maturity is not solely about reaching a particular milestone or finding success. It's not just the what but also the why and the how. Maturity is a measure of your internal dialogue, the variables you consider and evaluate prior to making a decision or taking action. The path is equally as important as the destination. Maturity is an understanding that your choices will impact others, and it's your responsibility to evaluate your decision making through the lens of those potential impacts.

Furthermore, much like the after-action reports I had to file in combat, your responsibilities do not end once the decision has been made. Every choice you make is an opportunity to learn if you evaluate the actual outcomes or the "truth data" of the effect your decision had on all other factors.

The fighter pilot community is excellent at driving self-evaluation and critique of personal performance. What my combat experience in Afghanistan taught me was the need to look beyond the immediate when conducting this evaluation. Learning from both your success and failures is critical for you to grow as a person. The more severe the impact, or the more intense the relationship, the more thought and consideration should be given before reaching a decision.

During my first deployment, I knew nothing personal about the men I killed and had no relationship with them, but the impact of my decision was the definition of severe. Back home, decisions I made that affected my family, while not life and death, were magnified significantly by the depth of my relationship with them. Knowing how to "get ahead" and live a life that looks good on paper will eventually fail to be enough.

The mental calculations it took to become a good pilot cannot be confused with the sacrifices necessary to be a caring husband and father or a better fighter pilot. Seeking more skill or being worried about what others thought about me were ultimately childish pursuits if doing so came at the detriment of my family or caused unreasonable harm to others around me.

When I began to look at the decisions I made in my personal and my professional life with the same broader perspective with which I was analyzing my combat missions, it made me a better father and husband, a better officer and fighter pilot.

Although this was a lesson I learned on the battle-field, thankfully combat is not a requirement to learn it. Very few people will find themselves making life or death decisions in their daily life, but everyone will be faced with choices that affect their loved ones and friends, their coworkers and acquaintances. As a true "adult," you have a responsibility to those affected by the decisions you make to ponder the potential ramifications, the costs and benefits of your choices before acting and to learn from the results of your decisions, regardless of the outcome.

---

### Popeye's Wisdom:

Maturing into an adult is not something that simply happens without conscious effort. The lessons provided by life experiences must be internalized before they can be translated into action.

Your decisions affect those around you, which gives you an obligation to consider the potential outcomes before acting and to learn from the results of your choices.

---

# GREG "FREDDY" KREUDER

Life is short. We are just passing through and have limited time to reach our goals. Plus, we are all works in progress and cannot learn without making mistakes. So, things don't always go the way we want them to, which can cause significant stress. By deliberately separating the few things we do control in life (attitude, preparation, effort) from the majority we do not (everything else), we can focus our efforts where they can make the most impact and not sweat the rest.

I certainly do not always get this right, but this technique has often helped me make a positive difference and maintain work/life balance without letting stress over things I cannot control get the better of me. I hope it can help you too.

# CHAPTER 7

# A FIGHTER PILOT'S PERSPECTIVE ON CONTROL

Regardless of badge or rank, as Airmen, we all decided to put the needs of our country above our own. We work in high-pressure environments where we compete with peers for jobs, schools, and promotions. Yet we still need to function as cohesive teams to achieve each of our squadrons' missions.

If we can't adapt, this leads to undue stress and friction. In this article, I'll offer a perspective gained during undergraduate pilot training as perhaps one way to strike a balance between these competing interests. In my 16 years in the Air Force since pilot training, I've truly enjoyed serving without concern for what the future holds. In my view, the issue of control is at the heart of the matter.

Whether or not we agree, most have heard the saying, *"Control is an illusion."*

*If true, should we throw our hands up in defeat?*

On the contrary, I propose we separate the few things that are within our control from the vast remainder which are not. We should expend our best effort where we can, and let the rest ride. It sounds simple, but this requires critical analysis and deliberate effort.

In my opinion, what we can truly control are two things: our effort, starting with preparation through execution, and our attitude. Pretty much everything else is outside our control.

By focusing on one and disregarding the other, I suggest we'll lead less-stressful lives and perform better. To a certain extent, I submit that stress is the manifestation of our inability to control events which, for whatever reason, are outside our control.

I graduated Officer Training School in 1995 and went to pilot training at Laughlin Air Force Base, Texas, where I flew the mighty T-37 Tweet, followed by the T-38 Talon.

It quickly became clear that this deliberate high-pressure environment would determine not only who could fly jets well but also who could deal with stressful situations. The reasoning is straightforward. The pressure cooker is designed to replicate the stress of say, an in-flight engine fire, without actually initiating one.

The Air Force needs pilots who react to emergencies in a cool, calm and professional manner, not someone who grabs the mic and yells, *"We're all gonna die!"*

As student pilots, we were graded on everything we did and how we did it, every day. Pilots who remained calm with a positive attitude invariably performed better than those who didn't.

Everybody has good and bad days, and I'm no exception to this rule. Although it's easy to be in a good mood when things go our way, the true measure of our character is when things don't go so well. For example, on one of my bad days, I left my trusty T-37's landing light extended when doing practice approach and landings at Laughlin Air Force Base, Texas.

After one particular approach, I failed to properly accomplish the checklist after bringing up the landing gear and completely forgot to retract my landing light. As I was about to overspeed the hapless appendage, my instructor took control of the aircraft and retracted it for me. He just as quickly handed me the aircraft back, and in the space of a few seconds, I knew I'd failed that sortie. Nuts!

As I walked home that afternoon, I asked myself if I had adequately prepared for the ride, put forth my best effort, and maintained a positive attitude throughout. These are the only variables truly within my control, and I strove to maintain the highest standard for each. Fortunately, in this case, I felt I maintained a positive attitude, was well-prepared, and did my best that day. This was an error in execution that happens to everyone from time to time. I didn't dwell on it and instead concentrated on the lesson: Stick to the checklist and retract the landing light, dummy!

The next day, I reflew the sortie without event and that was that.

Most Airmen in my class adopted a similar philosophy. Consciously or otherwise, we focused on having a good attitude and simply doing our best every day. We learned to let go of the rest, including the grades that ultimately determined class standing and our follow-on assignments. I'm confident we functioned well as a team due to this or a similar mindset. On occasion, thankfully rare, one of our classmates would excessively focus on grades and comparative class ranking.

This concentration on factors outside their control greatly increased the individual's stress and often soured that person's attitude. When the team members saw this, they joined forces and brought the wayward soul back on board. We taught each other to remain positive, focus on effort rather than performance on any given day, and let our instructors worry about how the rest would go.

The way I see it, there's only one person you have to prove anything to: *yourself.* I recommend we consciously "grade" ourselves by the few things we can control, such as preparation, effort, and attitude instead of how others see us—through grades, promotions, and ranking. Do the right thing because it's the right thing to do, and let our supervisors worry about performance reports and what our next jobs might be. For my part, this mindset has greatly reduced stress and allowed me to focus on what's important while truly enjoying the opportunity to serve in our Air Force. Although I wrote these thoughts down at the 16-year point in my career, they are just as true for me today as it was back then.

Although I've offered pilot training as an example, this approach can be applied to any environment where we work closely with one another yet are graded in relation to each other.

---

### Freddy's Wisdom:

Rather than focusing on the parts of control that remain an illusion, we can instead concentrate on the variables that occasionally drive the outcome in our favor. By doing so, we're maintaining full control of our sense of self-worth and ability to lead less-stressful and happier lives.

---

# TRENA "HAK" SAVAGEAU

"HaK" is a full-time wife and mom and part-time fighter pilot in the Air Force Reserve. She embraces the Air Force core values of integrity, excellence and service, and loves to share her fun, crazy stories about growing up as a girl in a male dominated field. She is proud to be an American and wants to inspire future generations to follow a calling of service.

*"Be who God meant you to be
and you will set the world on fire."*

**—St Catherine of Siena**

Email HaK at chickfighterpilots@gmail.com.

Facebook and Instagram: @chickfighterpilots

# CHAPTER 8

# A FLYING, FAILING SUCCESS

I'm a failure. But then again, so is every other fighter pilot; and I know none of us would ever want to change that.

As a cadet at the United States Air Force Academy, I was taught that the answer to any question was YES, SIR; NO, SIR; or NO EXCUSE, SIR. That was it. No whining, no explanations, no grey areas. I would win or I would lose. To an 18-year-old, it didn't make much sense, but over time, I would learn that this was the foundation of taking accountability for your actions—both in life and in flying.

I went to the Air Force Academy because I wanted to be an astronaut. At the time, the first step in reaching that goal required me to become a pilot, specifically a fighter pilot. Women were not allowed to fly fighters until 1994, my freshman year. Many people thought women wouldn't be able to handle the physical stressors of the G-forces or handle the possibility of being taken prisoner of war. I had instructors who told me I would never make it in a fighter squadron, never be accepted in that world. That message terrified me and nearly derailed my course. My first experience in a fighter squadron happened when I was a sophomore at the Air Force Academy. We visited Tyndall AFB, FL, and hung out with the F-15C pilots. It was meant to encourage us to choose flying fighters as a career. I left that trip with a bad impression of fighter pilots. As an outsider, the culture I witnessed was cutthroat and harsh. They laughed at the thought of a woman being successful in a fighter squadron. I was intimidated, and honestly, scared. I called my mom and told her fighter pilots were assholes and wanted nothing to do with that world.

But I had great people in my life that taught me never to back down from a challenge and to live my life with no regrets. And although it sucked sometimes, I grew up with two brothers who taught me how to fit in with the boys. Eventually, I earned myself a spot to pilot training, a scared second lieutenant hoping I didn't sign up for a decade-long commitment to something I didn't like. Putting aside my fears, I chose the risk. I chose to work hard, and I chose to try.

*What was the worst that could happen?*

Pilot training was extremely hard work, but I was ready and willing: 12-hour days in the squadron followed by hours studying at home and on weekends; working with classmates to memorize everything and visualize everything. We worked hard and played just as hard. I began to get my first taste of the pilot culture from the inside. I saw dedicated officers working their hardest every day, friendships built on shared experiences and failures, a little bit of "earned arrogance," and most important, humility. We found the road to being a fighter pilot was paved with daily, if not hourly, failures.

In pilot training, we started every day with "Stand -Up." We sat in a circle around the center of the room and were presented with an inflight emergency situation. One student was selected at random to stand at attention and recite the correct procedures to safely recover the aircraft and correctly answer any additional questions from the core of instructors sitting behind us. It was always nerve-wracking, praying you weren't the one to be called on. If you got anything wrong, a second person was called on to stand up and correct your mistake to finish the exercise. If that student failed, another was called on. This continued to the fourth or fifth student on some days! When we failed by answering something incorrectly, we were "grounded" for the day. "Grounded" in pilot terms, means we weren't allowed to fly but instead had to spend the day doing knowledge review and remedial training. It was embarrassing, but it happened to nearly everyone. Instead of folding under the pressure, we had to learn to find the silver lining, figure out where we went wrong and share lessons learned with our classmates. We learned to multiply our resilience by sharing the stories of our failures. NO EXCUSE, SIR! We learned to accept the consequences of our actions early, never a victim, always learning. Those that couldn't take accountability for their mistakes and failures often times didn't make it through training.

With God's help, I made it through with 13 of my Air Force brothers and selected the F-16 as my future. I wanted to fly the "Viper" (the nickname of the F-16 Fighting Falcon) because of the diversity of missions it offered. I wanted a future that required me to continue to learn, work hard, and keep my mind and body sharp and primed.

F-16 training was even more difficult than pilot training. Early on, I failed a flight because of a few bad landings; they were hard landings, slamming the jet into the runway instead of smoothly guiding the wheels to the concrete. In a fighter squadron, every pilot is given a callsign, an alter ego, by their squadron mates. This is the ONLY name anyone at work will ever call you. As a matter of fact, I don't even know the real first names of many fighter pilots!

Sometimes your callsign is a play on popular phases, but usually it's something that describes a mistake. In my case, the bad landings earned me the callsign "Slam." "Slam" would remind me, and everyone I flew with, of my failure that day. I had a choice: Let "Slam" define me, or pull myself up by the bootstraps and learn something from it. Eventually, I would laugh about those bad landings. More important, I would understand that I learned the most from my failures.

"Slam" didn't stick with me. I outran that callsign at my first operational fighter squadron after dozens of successful landings, only then to be named "HaK." I don't love my callsign but have embraced it nonetheless. "HaK" didn't stem from a mistake—or so I'm told—but from being girly in a fighter jock's world. To this day, I still have obnoxious pink flight gear, pencils, headscarves, flashlights, and publications bags; the guys will never steal them!

There would be many more failures in my fighter pilot career. In the impossible quest for perfection, we are always bound to fail. But failure is how we learn. Imagine how many things we would never learn if we didn't try out of fear of failing! In the fighter world, we are trained to make decisions quickly—our lives depend on it—and to be accountable for the results. This is what I have come to love the most about flying F-16s: accountability and how the entire team works together to get better by facing our mistakes. Accountability makes us embrace failures, not fear them.

A few months after I arrived at my first fighter assignment, F-16Cs at Cannon AFB, NM, my mom asked me if I was now one of those "asshole fighter pilots" I had described to her a few years earlier. After understanding that a fighter pilot's confidence is the result of years of hard work, self-sacrifice, and learning from mistakes, I had a completely different point of view. That swagger was hard earned! My fighter squadron was a home away from home. The men and women that I flew with were my brothers and sisters. We trusted each other with our lives and put our lives on the line nearly every day. I would have given my life for any one of them, just as I would now for my children. Not many people get to work in an environment that is this intense yet also feels like a family. In my opinion, fighter pilots are secret superheroes: callsign-wearing badasses in uniform and humble, hardworking Americans in their normal lives.

I sometimes joke that my entire career is a failure; I never became that astronaut I thought I wanted to be. I did, however, find my passion in the F-16 and the fighter pilot world. Once I fell in love with the Viper, I never wanted to leave.

*So did I really fail?*

*Or did I actually succeed?*

I can still see myself, an intimidated 22-year-old girl, jumping into the scary unknown—and I'm so glad I took that risk.

My plan, 23 years ago, was to serve a 9-year commitment and move on. However, I'm still flying the Viper—it never gets old. I will always be grateful for that scared 22-year-old who bravely chose this path. I now encourage any young, aspiring fighter pilot to give it a try.

*What's the worst that could happen? Failure?*

---

**HaK's Wisdom:**

Great risk has brought great reward but not without innumerable ups and downs. I refuse to let my failures define me; instead, I learn everything I can from each misstep.

---

# DAN "RUDY" FLETCHER

"Rudy" hails from Springfield, VA. He attended Virginia Tech where he met his better half, Diana. They have four lively kids that keep things interesting. Rudy started his military career in the Marine Corps as an AV-8B Harrier pilot then made the jump to the Air Force to fly F-16s.

*"... do all to the glory of God."*

**−1 Corinthians 10:31 (KJV)**

Email Rudy at danfletcher7@gmail.com.

# CHAPTER #9

# COMMUNICATION
# FOUNDATION

The British Empire faced an existential threat in the summer of 1940. Hitler had just completed his blitz across Western Europe and now turned his war machine upon the lonely island across the English Channel.

His plan was straightforward enough. Terror bomb the Brits into submission. Endless streams of Henkel bombers unleashed upon British cities would surely destroy their resolve. Hitler nearly achieved his objective. The British spirit began to wane in the face of seemingly endless capacity and destructive force of the Luftwaffe.

*How could this tiny island ever hope to survive against the juggernaut that had just destroyed all of their European allies? What hope could they have following their narrow escape at Dunkirk?* Some called for parlay with the Reich, but one man rallied a nation in its moment of greatest need.

Winston Churchill knew that repelling the Reich would take far more than tactics, technology, and troops. He would need to light a fire in the very soul of the British people. For that, Churchill turned to his most potent weapon: the spoken word.

On June 4, 1940, Churchill addressed the House of Commons with these immortal words, *"Even though large tracts of Europe and many old and famous States have fallen or may fall into the grip of the Gestapo and all the odious apparatus of Nazi rule, we shall not flag or fail. We shall go on to the end, we shall fight in France, we shall fight on the seas and oceans, we shall fight with growing confidence and growing strength in the air, we shall defend our Island, whatever the cost may be, we shall fight on the beaches, we shall fight on the landing grounds, we shall fight in the fields and in the streets, we shall fight in the hills; we shall never surrender..."*

There would be no question where the British stood following Churchill's call to arms. The Brits resolved to fight, and fight they did. British fighter pilots manned their fighters and single-handedly saved the nation in a brilliant and stunning victory over the mighty Luftwaffe. Churchill's oration was the driving force that inspired a nation to achieve victory against impossible odds, proving that spoken word is a mighty tool in the hands of those who know how to wield its power.

Effective communication is a compelling force whether briefing an alpha strike package, teaching young pilots tactical fundamentals, or even having a simple conversation with a friend. There are endless tools that can be leveraged to improve the potency of communication.

Humor, storytelling, vocal inflection, cadence, brevity, confidence, and physical presence are some of the skills that will enhance communication. These tools can be mastered, but more is required if one seeks to stir an audience. Truly great communication demands a firm foundation. Passion and purpose lay the groundwork for the kind of communication that will not simply convey information but stir souls as Churchill did on that historic summer day.

Passion is the cornerstone of great communication. If the speaker does not believe in their subject matter, it is impossible to reach their audience. This is why so many politicians' speeches fall flat. Their speeches are impeccably executed with every public speaking technique and oratory flourish, yet their audience remains unmoved. Passion is the crucial ingredient that they lack. Passion is a deep devotion to the subject matter and genuine desire to see their audience thrive.

Passion enables the speaker to connect with an audience that would otherwise be impossible.

Consider Dr. Martin Luther King Jr.'s speech during the March on Washington. Dr. King was appointed to make the case for equality to the American people. However, he did not simply delineate a series of goals or objectives. When he stood in front of the nation and declared, *"I have a dream that my four little children will one day live in a nation where they will not be judged by the color of their skin but by the content of their character,"* he spoke from the depths of his soul to the heart of the nation. Passion was the great power that Dr. King leveraged. Passion moved his audience. Passion was the stimulus that moved a nation to rise above the tyranny of racism. That same power is available to any speaker that would find their passion.

Great speakers appreciate the fact that their craft is not merely a talk with an audience, but part of a great endeavor to move their listeners to a higher purpose. Too often the purpose is lost. A lesson is more than the content at hand. A fighter pilot briefing is more than simply discussing how the mission is to be executed. A conversation is more than a discourse between two individuals. Simply presenting information, no matter how eloquently executed, without a clear objective is inevitably doomed to be forgotten as soon as the audience steps away from the speaker.

The subject matter must be driven by a deep and abiding purpose.

As Simon Sinek stated in *Start with Why*, "*People don't buy WHAT you do, they buy WHY you do it.*" People long to be moved to something beyond themselves. Therefore, the speaker must determine what is the ultimate purpose of their content. A lesson on military tactics is more than merely the mechanics, but a critical component in the defense of a great nation. Likewise, a flight brief is more than achieving success on a singular event, but serves to drive an individual one step closer to their higher calling. The speaker must be constantly assessing how their material compels their audience ever closer to their ultimate objective.

Neither the victory of Churchill nor the inspiration of Dr. King could ever have been realized without passion or purpose.

---

### Rudy's Wisdom:

Effective communication can only be built upon the firm foundation of a speaker who cares deeply about their content and drives their audience to a grand objective. Communicators must move beyond wrote presentation of information and allow their passion to drive their words and their purpose to inspire their audience.

---

# PATRICK "BAMBI" WHERRY

A graduate of the University of Washington in Seattle, "Bambi" joined the United States Marine Corps in 2005. After earning his wings of gold in 2008, his first assignment was flying the AV-8B Harrier with VMA-214 "Black Sheep" squadron in Yuma, Arizona. While there, he deployed with the 11th and 13th Marine Expeditionary Units onboard the USS Makin Island and USS Boxer. In 2014, Bambi moved to Cherry Point, North Carolina, to join VMAT-203 as a Harrier Instructor Pilot teaching new pilots to fly and employ the AV-8B. Transitioning to the USMC reserves in 2018, he continued to fly with VMAT-203 until 2020 when he transferred to the United States Air Force Reserve. He is currently assigned to the 69th Fighter Squadron as an F-16 B-Course Instructor Pilot at Luke Air Force Base, Arizona.

# CHAPTER 10

# COMFORT CONTAINERS

R aising children is easily one of the most reward-ing experiences one can ever have. It's fun, exhausting, scary, exciting, challenging, often over-whelming, and incredibly meaningful. Some people are born to be parents; some are apprehensive to start. Others are thrust into parenthood, yet all experience the same highs and lows. The same can be said for being an instructor pilot. Both are incredibly rewarding (while also creating grey hairs) and share the same end state: developing strong, contributing members of your community and ensuring its future success.

There are also similar tools and comparisons to be used to help make you effective at both. One of the most important things is to consider first what your own limitations and weaknesses are and how those limitations change as you gain experience.

First time parents with a newborn are different parents than ones with four kids aged two through twelve, but each have their own strengths and weaknesses. The same is true for instructor pilots; the environment we operate in as both parents and pilots is unforgiving of any incapacity, carelessness or neglect. *So how can we be successful and operate comfortably in these unforgiving and often hazardous environments?*

Consider your comfort level as a container. The container grows larger the more comfortable you are and shrinks smaller with stress and loss of confidence. As you are first learning to fly, your comfort container is small. You adhere strictly to rules, procedures and techniques taught to you by your instructors, and your likelihood to push any boundaries is small, which is a good thing.

As you learn more and become more proficient, your comfort container grows. This is also a good thing. It makes you a better, more confident pilot, and flying becomes even more fun. Learning happens faster, and your motivation goes up, which in turn makes you better. And your container continues to grow. At some point, your comfort will grow a little too much. Perhaps some complacency sets in, or you push a boundary, and you scare yourself. The size of your container is determined by the severity of your error. You operate a little more cautiously, and you've in turn gained some valuable experience. As you build more proficiency, your container begins to grow again and so on. This growing and shrinking of your comfort container continues throughout your career, and it forces you to constantly evaluate your skill level and makes you better.

The same thing happens as you begin to teach new pilots. Before you start instructing, you'll hear the horror stories of things that can go wrong with students, and you're convinced they're all trying to kill you. Your comfort container shrinks down. This is mostly for the better—a little bit of stress focuses our attention and keeps us sharp.

However, if your comfort level is too small, your student won't learn as well. You have to accept a bit of risk, and allow small mistakes, or learning will be stifled. No one likes to fly with the guy that rides the controls or talks constantly through every maneuver and phase of flight. The key is to decide how much error you're willing to accept for each part of the flight. Talk to the experienced instructors about common errors they've seen and what they accept. Then identify high-risk flight regimes, and try to quantify before the brief how much error you'll allow before starting any intervention.

After about a year or so of instructing, your comfort level will grow, and you'll have a pretty good grasp on how much error to allow to maximize student growth and learning. By year three, your comfort container likely will have grown too large; some complacency will inevitably set in, and you'll get surprised.

Perhaps a strong student will do something unexpected while you're complacent, but whatever the reason, your container will again be rudely snapped back to a smaller size. And you're again forced to evaluate where your instructional weaknesses are and adjust. The best way to prevent an inflated comfort container is to first identify the current status of your comfort level; *Is the container currently expanding or contracting?* Then stay engaged by trying to predict and anticipate the next error that will be made throughout the flight.

Parenting young kids is much the same. Try and identify the current status of your parental comfort container, and anticipate what will be the next blunder your child is going to make and how far you let them go before stepping in. We let our toddlers climb stairs but know they will likely fall and are there to catch them when they do. *Why does the third child get away with more than the first child did?* Perhaps our comfort container grew a bit too much, and we need to reevaluate our attentiveness and what risk we're willing to accept.

While we wouldn't go so far as to say that all people should be parents, all (good) pilots should strive to instruct in some capacity during their career. It may not seem as glamorous as some other endeavors, but raising the next generation—whether they be your biological children or the newest fighter pilots—is likely the most important thing you will ever do.

+++

*"There are many kinds of success in life worth having. It is exceedingly interesting and attractive to be a successful businessman, or railway man, or farmer, or a successful lawyer or doctor; or a writer, or a President, or a ranch man, or a colonel of the fighting regiment, or to kill grizzly bears and lions. But for unflagging interest and enjoyment, a household of children, if things go reasonably well, certainly makes all other forms of success and achievement lose their importance by comparison."*

**—Theodore Roosevelt (father of 6)**

---

**Bambi's Wisdom:**

The most talented pilots and parents are soon rendered worthless if they are unable to effectively communicate how they fly and share their knowledge with others to make their community better.

---

# KRISTOPHER "SWAT" HOLSTEGE

"Swat" is currently serving as an instructor and evaluator pilot at Luke Air Force Base, AZ, and has previously served time in combat units in Korea and Italy. As a former collegiate athlete, Swat relishes the opportunity to instruct and coach the next generation of fighter pilots who will leave Luke Air Force Base and join combat squadrons around the world.

*"If you ever see a turtle on a fence post, there is one thing you can be sure of. It didn't get there by itself."*

**–Coach Fisher Deberry**

Email Swat at Krisholstege@gmail.com.

# CHAPTER #11

# LIVIN' THE DREAM

So there I was, walking into the vault before a 0430 brief to lead a student sortie. As I was badging in, a sleepy-eyed lieutenant emerged from the man trap and said, *"Morning Swat, how you doin'?"* To which I replied, *"Livin' the dream, brother."*

He kind of smirked as if I was being sarcastic or cynical given the early morning brief. He might have even thought this was just my standard reply to people who ask me how I'm doing, and he would have been correct. However, it's not a lie. When people at work ask me how I'm doing, it's a meaningful response when I tell them I'm living my dream.

When I was six years old, my parents took me out to the Grand Rapids airport to see my first airshow. At this point, I had developed somewhat of an interest in military aircraft after having watched a VHS TV recording of *Top Gun* five or ten times. Actually, standing there on the ramp and looking at an F-14 and talking to the pilots turned the fictional world of *Top Gun* into a living, breathing reality to me. From that point on, I could not consume enough information about military aircraft. I was obsessed.

In the summer of 1989, my family took a vacation to Colorado. One of our day trips from Rocky Mountain National Park was down to Colorado Springs to visit the United States Air Force Academy. Seeing all the sights of the Academy, I had made up my mind. I was going to be a fighter pilot. When I returned to school that fall, my first-grade teacher assigned us to journal about what we did over the summer break. My journal entry detailed my experience in Rocky Mountain National Park and the Air Force Academy. It concluded with a single statement. *"When I grow up, I want to go to the Air Force Academy and become a pilot."*

Through elementary and middle school, I was the kid who already knew what he wanted to do with the rest of his life. Nothing could change my mind. I told every teacher, guidance counselor and coach that I wanted to go to the Air Force Academy.

My parents introduced me to another parent at my school who went to the Academy and was now in the Air National Guard flying A-10 Warthogs. He gave me some great advice. He told me to be a well-rounded person and take the opportunity to lead whenever possible. With that advice in mind, I started my quest.

In fifth grade, I started playing in the percussion section of the band. Through middle school, I played football, basketball, track and baseball. I competed in ski club in the winter and acted in the middle school play. I had two older sisters who gave me some solid advice about staying out of trouble and making smart decisions.

My dad and brother continually challenged me to grow as an athlete. In high school, I dropped baseball my freshman year and eventually ended up only doing football and track my junior and senior years. I continued playing in the percussion section of the symphonic band all four years of high school, and I was on student council all four years. I also volunteered to work with our students with special needs during my study hall period.

During my junior year of high school, a teacher stopped me in the hall and said, *"Hey Holstege, I took a look at your classes for next semester and noticed you hadn't signed up for advanced chemistry or precalculus. I know you're looking to get into the Air Force Academy, so I went ahead and changed your classes for you. If you don't want to go to the Academy anymore, you can change them back."*

I ended up being a fairly successful football player and track athlete competing for state championships in both. As such, I was recruited to play football at several Division II schools in the state of Michigan. However, the Air Force Academy had a Division I football program, so I decided to add this as the icing to my dream cake of going to the Academy.

I sent the football department a highlight tape in the winter of 2001 and waited to hear back. In the meantime, I had worked the admissions process and received a nomination to the Air Force Academy from my congressman. A few weeks later, I received a call from a coach at the Air Force Academy, and he said they wanted to start recruiting me to play football and asked a little more about my grades. I told him I had already received a nomination from my congressman and my package was with the admissions board at the Academy. Wouldn't you know it, that spring I received my appointment.

Prior to leaving to go to basic training, my mom had gone through some old papers and actually found my first-grade journal entry and put it on display next to my acceptance letter into the Academy. I was on my way. Little did I know, the easiest part was behind me, and life would bring a whole new level of challenges. I was challenged with basic training, freshman year, four years of football and majoring in Civil Engineering. None of these challenges were going to keep me from what happened on February 25, 2008. On this day, I strapped into the front seat of an F-16 fighter jet and took to the skies over Phoenix.

Now, I want to talk to you, the reader—another dreamer like myself. As I look back at this journey, I realize that there was one theme that kept me afloat through all of the challenges that I have faced, and it was an attitude of gratitude. My parents raised me to work for anything I'd ever wanted because no one was going to give it to me. It turns out the world is a network of individual experiences all waiting to be connected.

I made my dreams known, and the world around me came alive with people who were willing to help me out. People saw through my actions and gratitude that I was worth helping. No one owed me anything. I was not entitled to an appointment to the Academy, a spot on the football roster nor the pilot training slot after I graduated.

A lot of friends, family and acquaintances helped me out, and I owed it to them to make it worth their while. Having this *attitude of gratitude* gave me perspective whenever I faced disappointment or failure. When I didn't make the travel roster my sophomore year at the Academy, I was grateful for the friendships and leadership opportunities I had playing another year of scout team in practice.

This attitude of gratitude should not be confused with an attitude of apathy and accepting good as good enough. I wasn't happy just being on the team and getting a free meal. I owed it to those who helped me to work for that starting spot that I finally achieved my senior year.

---

### Swat's Wisdom:

If you want to live your dream, you have to be ready and willing to face the challenges and failures that come with your pursuit. No one owes you anything, but there are a lot of good people in this world that want to see you succeed. You just need to find them and tell them what you want and show them how bad you want it.

---

*"Aviation is proof that given the will, we have the capacity to achieve the impossible."*

**—Eddie Rickenbacker**

# MARK "KEGEL" ALLEN

Less than a year following the events of the story in this chapter, "Kegel" flew the Hog for the final time. He would go on to instruct Undergraduate Pilot Training at Laughlin AFB, Del Rio, Texas. There, he spent more than ten years attempting to master another aviation classic: the T-38 Talon. At Laughlin, he dedicated himself to passing on what he had learned to the next generation of Air Force and Allied Nation pilots. He retired in 2015 and now lives in Northern Arizona...and is still searching for all the answers.

Email Kegel at allen_mba@hotmail.com.

# CHAPTER 12

# READY WHEN IT MATTERED

*"Hawg 31, Bulldog Ops."*
*"Go."*
*"Call ready to copy...Troops in Contact."*

It was our second flight of the day and my tenth in a week and a half since arriving in Theatre. Combat-paired for the day, we were operating from Bagram AB in Northern Afghanistan.

As Ops relayed the coordinates and limited details of the situation to Lead, I scrambled through the contents of my saddle bag for the area map and feverishly plotted the location.

*"2 shows it within 1 klick of The Horseshoe."*
*"1, same. Call ready to taxi."*

**A few things *not* working in our favor:**

- Americans were under fire 100 miles away.

- We weren't flying the fastest machine ever.

- Sunset was approaching, and I hadn't gotten the NVG lights-out landing training.

**A couple of things we had going for us:**

- Coordinates were within a kilometer of a nameless bend in a river where we had been earlier that day. We'd spent over an hour talking (in fact whispering) back-and-forth with the task force that was intercepting a travelling enemy unit but now had been ambushed instead.

- Just like this morning, we were about to fly God's greatest gift to the American infantryman, the most lethal close air support machine ever constructed, the A-10 Thunderbolt II, "The Warthog!"

Based on our location, fuel state, and this morning's experience, there were no two people on earth more qualified to deal with the current situation. As we raced to the East and North, we attempted to gather updates along the way and listened-in on two squadron mates already working the problem. They'd had little success so far as they launched multiple marking rockets and attempted to get a good talk-on to the friendly position.

We listened closely, waiting our turn, as the Forward Air Controller (FAC) embedded with the friendlies attempted to explain their location and relationship to the enemy, both which were scattered about on a steep and rugged hillside. Not long after we arrived on scene, the previous 2-ship bingo'd out, leaving us with several problems: the FAC shouting over enemy machine-guns and friendly suppressing fire, a soon-to-be setting sun, and limited situational awareness of the precise enemy and friendly locations.

It seemed like nothing relayed back-and-forth over the radio made it any clearer how to separate the good guys from the bad. The mountain top was bathed in the dying light of day, and much of the craggy slope was obscured by deep shadows. This was the background from which we had to distinguish men trying not to be found from over ten thousand feet above.

Lead was hurrying as best he could, but nothing seemed to be working. We were, of course, following the first (unspoken) rule of close air support: Better to let the enemy kill the good guys than you do it for them. There was very little that was distinct, man-made, or had any contrast with the surrounding environment.

I listened intently to the frustrating conversation but couldn't glean anything useful. *"Are they in the sun or in the shade?"* Turns out, that was the key question which Lead relayed. Bad guys in the sunlight, good guys in the shade. Now we're in business.

Soon we were rolling in from the North dropping single, 500-pound bombs.

I was first to drop, a ball of nerves.

Pickle.

Climbing safe escape.

Hard right bank.

Splash.

Long pause...

*"Good bomb!'*

Relief.

After limited flying the past three months, I was within 1 kt of airspeed and 1 deg of dive of planned release parameters. Turns out, the muscle memory of hundreds of times down the chute in years past was there when I needed it.

Long hours of preparation for hundreds of training flights, late nights, early mornings, weather cancellations, briefings that never resulted in a mission, long debriefs of failures and the resulting repeated upgrade flights had all been distilled into these few moments. We cleaned up with long pulls of the gun, and it was time to return to base (RTB). He laughed with relief when we asked for bomb damage assessment (BDA). *"It's not like there are dead bodies lying around all over the place!'*

That was my most impactful and significant sortie as an A-10 Hog Driver.

I'll always remember the faces of my crew chief who handed me the rings and streamers from the heavy weights that we had dropped, my squadron friends in Kuwait who were happy to see someone on the B team come through when given a chance, and my bosses back home who wanted to hear all the details after we had returned to Tucson weeks later.

I really did some reflecting about what happened that day and what it meant. It bothered me that we hadn't heard back about how it all ended. It had been a significant emotional event in my life, and it had to have been for those guys on the ground.

*Why hadn't we heard?*

Later, when relating this story to one of my squadron-mates, I tried to get all the details right but told him that we had never heard back or officially found out what happened to the good guys on the ground, no mission report (MISREP), no BDA. It turns out the guy I was telling had been in Al Udeid in Theater Headquarters at that time and was somewhat familiar with the situation.

He said that those we supported that day were probably from Task Force 180-something or other, three letter agencies involved, and that they were unlikely to file such reports, or the reports that they did file didn't filter back down to people in lofty positions such as my own!

Despite no concrete details of the results of the weapons we employed, what I do know with confidence was what it sounded like when the guy on the radio was whispering that morning, and what it sounded like when they were frantically attempting to confirm positions of friend and foe with gunfire in the immediate background, and again at the end when he laughed with obvious relief.

I'll never know for sure, but I believe things would have been significantly different had we not been there that day. I like to think that there are men walking the earth today and children that were born later because the two of us were there, on that day, at that time. Maybe some kid grew up to know his father or could play ball with his dad because we were there, at that time, when it mattered, to make the critical difference.

That's my story...and I'm sticking to it.

+++

Dedicated to my father, Donald Allen. Youngest of five, a graduate of Colorado A&M in Mathematics. Drafted into the Army during the Korean War, part of a small New Mexico unit studying yields of nuclear and thermonuclear weapons. Later worked for Sandia Corporation, TRW, Aerospace Corporation and Aerojet Electrosystems in a career spanning nuclear weapons, ICBMs and defense satellites from Korea through Desert Storm. Survived life-saving surgery at two days old, passed away 86 years later, 13 years after a stage 4 lung cancer diagnosis. A fighter from start to finish.

Rest in Peace.

---

**Kegel's Wisdom:**

Maybe not in the grand scheme of human events or history, but in the lives of a few brave men caught in a tough situation, we made a key difference. In my own life, I was thankful and able to rest easy knowing that when I was called upon, the one time when my country needed me, when my brothers needed me, when it really mattered...I was ready.

# J. BRYSON "DIRTY" BYRD

"Dirty" is an F-35 instructor pilot in the 60th Fighter Squadron at Eglin AFB, FL. He hails from Orlando, FL, graduated from the University of Arkansas, and got his commission through Officer Training School (OTS). He is a former F-16 instructor pilot of the USAF Weapons School. In 2018, he started a side career in real estate as a REALTOR® in both Alabama and Florida. "Dirty" and his wife, Melissa, recently started a business managing vacation rental properties in Destin, FL.

*"Humility is not thinking less of yourself, but thinking of yourself less."*
**–C.S. Lewis**

Email Dirty at afterburnervrllc@gmail.com.
Visit his site: https://jamesbyrd.exprealty.com.

# CHAPTER 13

# THE ART OF THE FIGHTER PILOT DEBRIEF

As I look back on the memorable people I've met, the ones that made the biggest impression on me had something in common: the **Desire to Win!**

I've found and cultivated some amazing friendships with nonpilots, but I still find myself left with the same conclusion: *Why are an overwhelming amount of fighter pilots successful?*

I'm not implying that success is a byproduct of flying fighter jets for a living, but I can't look beyond the evidence that most fighter pilots are successful at life. American fighter pilots are accustomed to winning and embody some general characteristics: well-educated, smoking hot spouses, beautiful and brilliant children, financially thriving, etc.

*Why is that?*

*What do fighter pilots do that sets them apart from the rest?*

It's simple—they've learned the art and importance of a **Fighter Pilot Debrief**.

If you are even remotely familiar with fighter jets, Hollywood's *Top Gun* legacy, or classic documentary shows like *Wings* or *Dog Fights*, you've probably heard of briefing and debriefing. In essence, a day of flying fighters looks like this: We talk about what we're going to do, we go do what we said we were going to do, and then we talk about what we just did. In other words, plan, brief, execute, and debrief.

The majority of sorties in a fighter squadron are generated to support qualification upgrades, which results in young fighter pilot mistakes. I was given the opportunity to teach in the Air Force's doctorate-level Weapons School as an F-16 instructor pilot. Our typical student syllabus missions involved an eight-to-ten-hour planning day, a two-hour mission briefing, a one-hour flight, and a four-to-six-hour debrief—all depending on the complexity and phase of the course.

If you are bad at math in public, we're only physically piloting the F-16 Viper for 5% of the time; 95% of our effort is consumed with other tasks. Yes, 5%, one hour of flying for every eighteen hours of chit-chat.

In the words of Jack Donovan, one of the original Wild Weasels, *"You gotta be shittin' me!"*

*So, what then?*

Fighter pilots talk a lot; if you came to that conclusion, you're not wrong! We'll tell you about our jets and then tell you about ourselves, but it's not a matter of arrogance but a matter of confidence and satisfaction.

Here's the secret—fighter pilots take the 95:5 rule well beyond destroying surface-to-air missiles (SAMs), hardened targets, and advanced enemy fighters. We apply the 95:5 rule in nearly every single decision in our lives. It's a mindset and problem-solving methodology that becomes so ingrained that we do it subconsciously.

Suffice to say, the 95:5 rule is merely a label on the amount of forethought and planning that goes into our decision-making processes. In my opinion, every decision requires a cost-benefit analysis. Fighter pilots dwell on, and survive by, cost-benefit analyses.

To go one layer deeper, the single most important portion of the flying day is the Debrief. It's where we improve and learn. It's where self-betterment happens, and many times, it's a painful process that we find necessary to enable our future success. This is our most basic (and effective) debrief methodology:

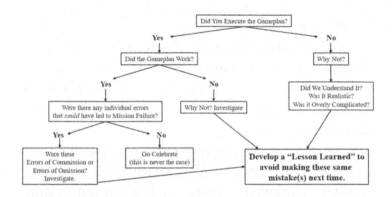

## Debrief Methodology

*So, how can you adopt this methodology in order to become successful?* What have I learned that has become invaluable to my success? I practice miniature self-debriefs to explore significant decisions made throughout the day. That means I intentionally carve out mental space to have a dialogue with myself.

I have a 25-minute commute to work and use this time to make assessments. In other words, *"Dirty, how did we do today?"* As an instructor, the majority of my mini self-debriefs revolve around my students' performance. I utilize the above methodology to measure the effectiveness of my instruction.

*First, did I have an intentional student development plan tailored to the student?*

*Did I execute that instructional plan?*

*Did that instructional plan work?*

Typically, I find that my effectiveness is dependent on my personal communication and interaction with the student instead of my technical expertise. That's what makes instruction so beautiful! It's not about what you know; it's about how you convey what you know.

The previous example is how I conduct a self-assessment for flying fighter jets, but I make it a point to utilize the same methodology for my relationships. I use the morning drive to reflect on the evening prior and assess my effectiveness as a Christ follower, husband, father, son and friend.

This is very important—highly successful people run an inherent risk of self-centeredness. I personally fall victim to that pitfall every day, but I'm also aware of the trap, which helps me include it in my self-betterment. Suffice to say, when you have a subconscious desire to be "the best" and outperform your peers, you need to "check your heart" (as my wife says) in your pursuit of success.

As a final thought, I think that fighter pilots are inherently successful for a lot of reasons, but the single most profound character trait I see in the truly successful is their desire to be the best. As previously mentioned, the pursuit of being superior comes with checks and balances of character.

However, convincing yourself that you can get better results than someone else is the underlying thrust behind success.

You simply cannot ever settle for mediocrity.

You should never be satisfied with below-average performance.

If you're going to do something, do it right, to the best of your ability, and to completion.

Debrief yourself.

In the words of my late friend and F-16 wingman, Captain William "Pyro" Dubois, *Moderation is for cowards.*

---

**Dirty's Wisdom:**

1. Desire to be the best at whatever you do.

2. Take time each day for mini debriefs in your personal and professional life.

3. If you are going to do something, take the time to do it right the first time.

4. If you fail, debrief yourself, and press on to win harder the second time.

---

*"Flying is more than a sport and more than a job; flying is pure passion and desire, which will fill a lifetime."*

**—Adolf Galland**

# MONESSA "SIREN" BALZHISER

"Siren" is a fighter pilot, wife, and mother who currently works as a Lockheed Martin F-16 and F-35 company pilot. She has more than 15 years of flying experience around the world in both the military and corporate enterprise. Siren has been featured by multiple media outlets, including the BBC, NBC, UK's *FLYER* magazine, and *WarriorMaven.com*, to share her lessons learned from operational experiences and how to apply them to life situations–in and out of the jet. When not flying, Siren loves traveling, coffee, and DIY home projects. She lives in Fort Worth, TX, with her husband (also an F-16 pilot) and their daughter.

*"Continuous effort—not strength or intelligence—
is the key to unlocking our potential."*

**–Winston Churchill**

# CHAPTER 14

# "JUST BE A GOOD DUDE"

These five words create a simple phrase but carry a lot of meaning; it was a phrase that a friend and fallen fighter pilot often said during our time together in an operational fighter squadron in Japan.

*What does it mean to "be a good dude"?*

One can interpret the context of this phrase in a multitude of ways, but for me, being a "good dude" centers around a person's emotional intelligence, or EQ (emotional quotient). Considered the sibling to intelligence quotient (IQ), emotional intelligence is the ability to understand, use, and manage your own emotions in positive ways, and it is commonly defined by four key skills:

1) Self-management.

2) Self-awareness.

3) Social awareness.

4) Relationship management.

These skills are evolving elements of one's individual and social development. As such, they can be developed during any stage in life. Through utilization of EQ, people can communicate more effectively, empathize with others, overcome challenges, and defuse conflict.

In the fighter pilot community, most pilots tend to shy away from talking about feelings or emotions. The reason is not because of fear of ridicule or no need for an outlet, but rather an understanding among fighter pilots of what is required to succeed in this challenging profession.

Most fighter pilots have a high EQ because of their ability to control their emotions as well as read other's emotions, especially during high-stress and dynamic situations. A perfect example of fighter pilots utilizing the four common EQ skills is flying the number 3 position of a 4-ship formation.

When a 4-ship of fighters fly as a single formation and team, each person in the formation is tasked with certain responsibilities. The flight lead (#1) is charged with executing the overall game plan and ensuring mission objectives are achieved. The two wingmen (#2 and #4) support the game plan by flying the briefed formation, setting their sensors correctly, and taking care of contracted responsibilities, which may involve the important task of shooting the gun, dropping bombs, or firing missiles. The fighter pilot flying as #3 manages their own element (#3 and #4) in ways to maximize support for #1's game plan and does so in ways to enhance mission success.

The #3 position is challenging because the element lead not only carries the burden and responsibility of #1 by overseeing mission objectives but also needs to have the whereabouts to know when to speak up or deviate from flight lead's game plan. A good #3 must have the confidence and awareness to execute a different game plan if needed but without derailing #1's leadership or control—in doing so, he or she demonstrates substantial social awareness and relationship management.

A well-balanced #3 must further apply self-awareness and social awareness to perceive cues and recognize the formation's dynamics while communicating with the team to manage roles and potential conflict. In order to apply all these emotional intelligence skills, #3 must have a solid foundation of self-awareness and control. Subtly nudging #1 in the right direction if needed without usurping formation direction cannot be done by a #3 who does not understand and empathize with their formation lead's position.

Emotional intelligence does not only apply to flying—it can also pertain to any situation. How a person conducts themselves within the team, organization, or a large corporation, demonstrates their level of EQ, whether it comes naturally for that person or is learned over time. Most people can easily identify a person with a high EQ—often they are the individuals we seek out when building a team or from whom we ask advice.

They are usually the people at ease with themselves and their environment, creating a steady emotional force of stability and confidence. It is no different in a fighter squadron. Even in an environment filled with Type-A, motivated, and goal-oriented professionals, those with high EQs stand out as the most trusted, reliable, and levelheaded of the group who get the job done when it matters—and can do so without stepping on their peers or introducing negative group dynamics.

Everyone is still on their team. As a result, they often subsequently find themselves in leadership positions. In a fighter squadron, these may not be the pilots with the best technical flying skills or most awards, but rather they are the trusted peers that moderate the social dynamic, unite the squadron, and set the example. By exhibiting strong EQ, these individuals shape organizations and exert positive influence across large groups.

One pilot who flew as #3 multiple times in my formations embodied the four skills of emotional intelligence. His name was Stephen "Cajun" Del

Bagno, and not only did he encourage us all to "just be a good dude," he also embodied it as a fighter pilot and a person. Even though he's no longer with us, that phrase still consistently reminds me how important EQ skills can be and how equally important it is to continually develop them.

---

**Siren's Wisdom:**

Just be a good dude.

---

# DOUG "ODIE" SLOCUM

"Odie" is a 35-year career fighter pilot with more than 4,100 hours flying F-4, F-16, and A-10 aircraft. His last assignment before retiring in 2019 was as the 127th Wing and Installation Commander at Selfridge ANGB in Michigan. He is a well-known motivational speaker having given more than 750 presentations on safety and leadership to more than 150,000 attendees across the Air Force and more. His successful leadership style/philosophy is branded as *Violent Positivity*.

*"Above all, we must realize that no arsenal, or no weapon in the arsenals of the world, is so formidable as the will and moral courage of free men and women. It is a weapon our adversaries in today's world do not have."*

**–Ronald Reagan**

# CHAPTER #15

# VIOLENT POSITIVITY

I was blessed to wear the uniform of this country for over 35 years. It took a while for me to truly understand a very important concept; It's always about people. During my amazing journey, I developed a leadership philosophy that I ultimately branded as *Violent Positivity.*

*So why "Violent"?*

To paraphrase Clausewitz, *"War is merely the continuation of politics with other means."* The "other means" in this case being violence. "Violence" in the Merriam-Webster Dictionary in this application is "a vehement feeling or expression" not physical harm. While "passion" or "intense" are good synonyms, the word "violence" gets people's attention.

If someone challenges my word choice, I just paraphrase Harold Lasswell: We're in the military;

our job is the "management of violence," and then I smile.

As for "Positivity," I'll obscurely quote the Urban Dictionary to define positivity as *"staying positive even when you find a really good reason to be negative."*

Today, we have way too many examples and role models of negativity. Negativity has become our society's normalized deviancy. I think that's part of the magic of positivity. It catches people off guard. For the most part, they don't expect it or quite know what to do with it. It's new; it's refreshing.

It's amazing to see how well people respond to positivity. The secret ingredient of "Violent Positivity" finds its roots in what's known as the Pygmalion effect.

This simple and proven phenomenon is the law of self-fulfilling prophecy of expectations. Other's expectations can affect a person's performance. Here's how it works.

If you tell someone they're good, they eventually are going to think that they're good, which means they are going to act like they're good, and the result is that they will ultimately improve. In other words, you plant the seed, it germinates, it takes root, and eventually it finds the sun—and then it blossoms. To make it visual, take a look at the chart on the next page.

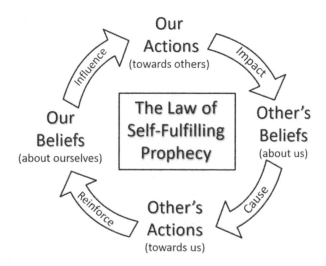

The opposite is also true and is known as the Golem effect. Negativity and low expectations result in poor performance. I think we can all recall a hurtful comment or put down from our past. It sticks, endures, and festers. An environment of low or unknown expectations lowers morale and decreases productivity. If you add in negative expectations, the environment and the culture can quickly turn toxic.

*So why not flip the script on toxicity and negativity and drive an optimistic organizational culture focusing on encouragement?* Here are some basics of operationalizing *Violent Positivity.*

**1. Start with names.** Learn names, use names, make eye contact, and call a person by their name. If you're not good at names, too bad. Work at it and overcome your aversion; don't be lazy. People have a physiological reaction to hearing their own name. It activates positive behaviors and thought patterns of core identity, and it drives attention to you and what you're saying. It also communicates familiarity and demonstrates that you care. Learning and using names is powerful.

**2. Be genuine and be humble.** If you want to serve and lead people, they need to see you as honest and approachable. The word I like best is vulnerable. Being vulnerable is not comfortable. It is, however, a decision—your decision. So many times, as leaders, we want to be seen as tough and emotionless. That has its place. But its application is few and far between. I have seen the best results from telling non-controversial or divisive stories about myself others can relate to.

*The easiest examples?*

Pets and family. *Who doesn't like a good story about a pet or a child?* This is one reason it's handy that I carry pictures of my daughter and my fur-babies around with me. Once you share your story, ask about theirs.

*The result?*

Instant connection and familiarity.

**3. Be a person of integrity.** In your brain, you know what's right and what's wrong. That's called your character. *Do your actions and behaviors accurately reflect your character?* Your integrity is that imaginary cable that connects your character with your conduct. As a leader, people watch everything you do both on and off the job—that includes social media. Your actions and behaviors become the standard. When it comes to integrity, you don't get a second chance. Once someone perceives that you've misled, lied, or not walked the talk, you have lost credibility as a leader. Model correct behavior in your personal and professional life—always.

**4. Value failure.** Let me say it again emphatically; value, treasure, and revel in failure. Every path to success has a trail of failures showing the way. It's normal to fail when you try something for the first time. If you want to be an organization where people reach new levels of performance or innovate to cutting-edge solutions, people need to be encouraged to try and try again. If they fail, have a celebration of the effort. Encouragement breeds excellence. Make a choice. Let people try. Let people fail. Then high-five the effort, and help them try again.

**5. Choose your words wisely.** Now I've circled back to the law of self-fulfilling prophecy. People will perform to the level of expectation and encouragement expected of them. Word choice and attitude matter. Each time you speak, your words leave an indelible imprint. Even in tough situations or confrontations, calm and kind words can solve what yelling and demands never will. The most powerful and influential voice is rarely the loudest.

In teaching leadership through the years, I always liked to ask a simple and philosophical question. *"If I took away your ability to reward or punish your employees, would they still want to follow you?"*

*If not, then why not?*

+++

**To contact Odie:**

LinkedIn: Doug "Odie" Slocum

Facebook: Doug Slocum (Odie)

---

**Odie's Wisdom:**

One person can make a profound difference in an organization. *Why not you?*

The bottom line—Violent Positivity can lead you and your organization to new levels of excellence.

*"Both optimists and pessimists contribute to our society. The optimist invents the airplane and the pessimist the parachute."*

**–Gil Stern**

# CHRIS "MULLIGAN" MARSLENDER

"Mulligan" is a command pilot with over 2,300 hours in the F-16 and F-35, including three deployments and over 500 combat hours. Lieutenant Colonel Marslender is a graduate of the United States Air Force Academy, United States Air Force Weapons School, and Naval War College. Upon completing a tour as Commander of the 56th Training Squadron, he relocated to the Eisenhower School for National Security and Resource Strategy in Washington, D.C.

*"Everyone makes mistakes.*
*The best don't repeat them."*

**–Chris "Mulligan" Marslender**

# CHAPTER #16

# SO THERE I WAS

W*hat do military operations, flight in fighter jets, and most life events all have in common?* They all require planning.

Depending on the event's complexity and risk, you may spend hours or even days planning. (Major military operations sometimes require weeks of planning.) Simple errands occasionally require some planning. Think about the last time you went to the grocery store. Even if you didn't make a list, you had a basic plan in mind of items to purchase. However, this is where life events and a brief trip down the aisles of your local store differ. Life often works out differently than your plan may have intended. This generality doesn't mean failure is rampant, but it does mean the following two rules are essential:

1) The military strategist, Carl von Clausewitz, famously stated, *"Only the element of chance is needed to make war a gamble, and that element is never absent."* Random events will almost always play out differently than you might have envisioned.

2) That doesn't mean your planning was a waste. It does mean you need to consider contingencies in your planning and be ready to change the plan on the fly. In the face of unforeseen adversity, you must summon your knowledge and adapt to the situation.

A brief story: So there I was, over the skies of Iraq in my F-16 fighter jet. That day, I led a formation of two F-16s. I was also the mission commander for twenty-four friendly fighter aircraft from three different countries. We were to attack several known hostile assets. Still, we were required to visually sanitize the targets to ensure no civilians were present before employing our weapons. We had a good plan, and everyone had a thorough understanding of their role. My 2-ship was the first to get fuel from the tanker about a hundred miles from the target area. As we finished refueling, a 4-ship was already in position to start their refueling, and multiple other formations were ready to get fuel after them. I directed our formation to the target area and immediately noticed the layers of cloud obscuration covered all targets.

On this particular day, some friendly aircraft planned to drop bombs that required them to see the target visually. My wingman and I arrived at the target area and circled a few times to find a gap in the clouds. We had briefed several contingency plans but had not discussed solid weather from eight to fifteen thousand feet over the target. Chance had injected an unforeseen and critical element into our mission. So, we adapted!

To visually clear the targets for civilians, I directed my wingman to stay visual, go to a clearing formation, and follow me. I then led our formation below the lousy weather to a point where we could see all the targets. I sanitized a few targets and briefly climbed us back into the clouds to avoid highlighting our position and receiving enemy fire. We repeated this several times until we had sanitized all the target areas.

Once the friendly fighters arrived, those dropping munitions requiring visual acquisition reported immediately they could not see their targets. Once again, I altered the plan on the fly and adapted to the current conditions. I redirected the final attack heading from an area where the cloud ceiling was slightly higher. I then asked the attacking formations to report different positions from the target, allowing me to find them on my radar and fly into position to guide their bombs. For the next forty minutes, my wingman and I repeated this process for our allied fighters: circled the target in the weather and timed our descents below the clouds to guide friendly bombs, none of which we had planned. We then employed our munitions on undestroyed targets. At the end of the strike, our strike package successfully destroyed all targets, and all fighter aircraft returned to their respective bases. The mission represented a first-time event for three countries and successfully demonstrated our ability to integrate with our allies.

The real point of this story is this: Adversity and changing conditions are nothing to fear. The most dynamic of scenarios are the times we, as a nation, have risen to the top. Even General Washington's fearless Christmas Eve nighttime assault across the Delaware River was a product of quick and adaptive innovation. Changing conditions and innovative, reactive thinking can be leveraged to improve your position.

Understand the value of planning. Reacting to chance and random events without a plan will not consistently work out in your favor. This foolish endeavor is akin to the difference between gamblers and poker players: One has dedicated significant study and practice; the other has not. The most prepared executors have considered multiple itera-tions and possible outcomes. Thus, even when condi-tions change to something you have not considered, you have already rehearsed extemporaneous thought. This mental exercise is the actual value of contingency planning.

Smooth skies and good luck!

---

### Mulligan's Wisdom:

1. As Benjamin Franklin suggested, *"A failure to plan is planning to fail."* Make a plan, and include consideration of how to react when things do not go according to plan.

2. Helmuth von Moltke taught the famous line, *No plan survives first contact with the enemy.* Be ready for your first flight in a fighter jet, your first challenging experience, or life in general to take a turn you had not anticipated. Chance rewards the prepared over the ill-informed or hopeful.

3. Roll with the punches. Revel in the challenge. Enjoy the ride, adapt, and overcome.

The best-laid plans do not always pan out. At the end of a challenge, the only requirement is that you can rest easy knowing you made the best decision with the information you had at the time and did not compromise any of your moral principles in the process.

# JEFF "TUCK" COHEN

"Tuck" served a 20-year career in the U.S. Air Force flying the mighty F-16. Between five operational duty assignments, he logged 2,600 hours of fighter time with over 500 combat hours. His assignments included stateside and overseas locations to include instructor duty at the USAF Weapons School. He culminated his career as a squadron commander at Misawa Air Base, Japan, where he led his squadron on a six-month combat deployment tasked against the Islamic State in Iraq and Syria. He was awarded the 2015 Clarence H. Mackay Trophy recognizing the most meritorious flight of the year across the entire U.S. Air Force. After retiring from active service in 2017, he lives in Wilmington, NC, with his wife and three children.

Email Tuck at cohenski@gmail.com.

# CHAPTER 17

# BREAKING THE RULES

O n a sunny day in early May 2015, I found myself in my F-16 fighter jet, 18,000 feet above northern Syria. Flying from a remote desert base, my wingman and I were tasked with destroying Islamic State positions close to friendly ground forces near the Turkish border. During this mission, I decided to break the rules.

As a U.S. Air Force F-16 fighter squadron commander, I often referred to this experience when talking to pilots before their first sortie in my squadron. I told all pilots under my command how important it was to follow rules and regulations on every flight. These rules and regulations, "written in blood," covered most situations—but not all. I also explained that, on rare occasions, circumstances dictated breaking the rules.

The dynamic ground situation in northern Syria that day in May 2015 meant that a controller thousands of miles away in the United States developed targets and directed attacks in real time. Despite a crackly and barely audible satellite radio, our controller helped us aim our sensors and weapons at enemy positions. Over three hours and three trips to the refueling tanker, we delivered seven precision bombs with devastating effects. The standard weapons load was four bombs per aircraft. With one remaining bomb, we headed to the tanker for the fourth time that day.

Low on gas, I opened my F-16's air refueling door. Despite several attempts, the tanker boom operator was unable to connect to my jet, probably due to a mechanical malfunction. I maneuvered to the side of the tanker while my wingman fueled up. Based on our location and my low fuel, I knew I could not make it back to our base. I would have to divert somewhere closer. And the divert options weren't good.

The only viable place to land was the airport at Erbil, a large city in northeastern Iraq. There, a skeleton American presence facilitated cargo aircraft movements. Fighter aircraft rarely landed there. After safely landing, my wingman and I taxied to an isolated transient parking ramp. Several Air Force cargo aircraft mechanics and crew chiefs were staring at us. Shutting down my jet's engine, I noticed the bare bones facilities. I thought, *"How am I going to get out of here?"*

Normally, when a mechanically wounded aircraft lands, experienced fighter jet mechanics fix it. The mechanics in front of me were only trained to repair cargo aircraft. Although they had general aircraft maintenance knowledge, they didn't have the tools, training, or certifications to work on my F-16. Neither did I. While renowned worldwide for our airborne death-dealing expertise, Air Force fighter pilots do not fix damaged airplanes.

*But what could it hurt to look?* I climbed on top of my F-16 and inspected the air refueling door and associated hardware components. I found a stuck component that prevented refueling on the ground and in the air. My jet was "Code 3," not airworthy until repaired. Air Force rules required that certified Air Force F-16 mechanics diagnose and repair the problem.

The Air Force is a rule-following organization. Countless pages of regulations outline rules for aircraft maintenance and flight operations. The "by the book" answer for my predicament was to call for help and wait. In peacetime, we would have waited twenty-four hours for a repair team to arrive. Due to the logistics in the combat world in which we operated, it would take three to four days for the mechanics and equipment to arrive. This delay would lead to significantly fewer combat sorties generated from our base. I was not willing to accept that.

Using a crew chief's cell phone, I called my maintenance leadership back at our base. They connected me to our top fuel system specialist. On top of my F-16 again, I described the situation to the fuel specialist, and he talked me through the repair that allowed on-the-ground refueling.

With a flathead screwdriver and limited assistance from the local cargo aircraft mechanics, I removed two jammed components—a fuel cap and a spring-loaded cylinder. Getting them back into the jet proved difficult. We struggled for forty-five minutes to compress the spring to engage the fuel cap's threaded screw. I was finally able to compress the spring enough to thread the cap into place. Seeing a solid seal, I judged the F-16 airworthy for our flight back to base.

Pilots never make this call for their own aircraft. Normally, only a qualified F-16 mechanic would have completed this repair. A supervisor would then have inspected the work and returned the aircraft to flight status. However, on that day, I broke the rules and declared the F-16 as airworthy.

And it was not the last rule I broke. We were rapidly approaching the maximum number of hours in our flight duty day. By the time the fuel truck arrived and topped off my F-16, we needed a waiver to fly a longer day. My commander, who could have approved more hours, was in "legal rest" status; he could not be disturbed. Unable to obtain a waiver, I presumed approval and decided to return to base. My wingman and I took off for an 800-mile flight, no air refueling needed. Our maintenance team was thrilled to get our jets back and quickly returned them to combat service.

Reflecting on this experience reinforced lessons learned in the Air Force. Remember that rules were written to account for most circumstances. When regulations do not fit circumstances, rely on judgment and experience for guidance. I decided that fixing the jet by the book was not a good option. Fixing my own aircraft and presuming I would get a waiver on exceeding the maximum flight duty day was the best call. Vindication came: No one questioned my decisions to break the rules.

General Douglas MacArthur cynically said, *"Rules are mostly made to be broken and are too often for the lazy to hide behind."*

---

### Tuck's Wisdom:

I suggest instead: Mostly, follow the rules. And—on rare occasions when rule following is counterproductive—think for yourself and act accordingly.

---

# DOMINIC "SLICE" TEICH

"Slice" is a Catholic man, husband, father, investor, business owner, entrepreneur, author, fighter pilot, and the founder of Single Seat Mindset. He understands that having a plan that lets you reach your biggest goals is paramount to your success. As a struggling peak performer, he understands this challenge well and pledges to help others experience professional and personal success by connecting them with other high achievers. Slice started the Single Seat Mindset Insider's Circle for goal-oriented individuals that want cutting-edge ideas and results in one place. We are all just little kids inside; being a fighter pilot lets me wear my onesie every day.

*"Learn to give and you will learn to live."*

# CHAPTER 18

# ARE YOU READY?

*"Viper 2, recover."*
*"Viper 2, check Aux."*

*"Viper, knock it off."*
*"Viper 1, knock it off."*

LONG PAUSE

*"...Viper 2, knock it off."*

So there I was...a blistering afternoon, 16,000 feet, strapped inside a single seat fighter jet over south Texas fighting my sixth high-aspect dogfight when I experienced one of the most shocking experiences of my life.

G-induced loss of consciousness...a violent fighter pilot nap that is unwelcomed and usually results in death.

## The Backstory

At 25 years old, I was in peak physical shape. My wife had finished nursing school, and we were pregnant with our first child. It was an exciting time flying fighter jets, and we were starting a family. I was an avid cyclist and logged about 5,000 miles a year even with a heavy work schedule.

I was on top of my game and physically fit; or at least I thought I was.

*Was I ready?*

## My Desire

My dad and I built a model F-4 fighter jet on my 7th birthday, and I convinced myself that one day I'd be a fighter pilot. The status, identity, and subconscious drive to fly single seat fighter jets and "be one of them" kept me going throughout my childhood, into college, as a civilian flight instructor, and finally as a real fighter pilot.

At times, it seemed impossible. Frustration, fear, and a feeling that I might not have what it takes was hard to shake...but I pressed on.

My false beliefs were shattered in college when I met fighter pilots that taught aviation classes. They told me, *"Hell, kid, I did it. Why can't you?"* That was the first real step in my young adult life when I mentally recommitted to the possibility that it could happen.

That could be me.

Maybe if I tried hard enough, studied, applied myself, stayed out of trouble, and mixed in a little luck, I could be one of them someday.

I was committed and went all in on my plans to fly fighter jets.

With hyperfocused effort and good timing, my plan worked. I found myself strapped into the ejection seat prior to taxiing for takeoff thinking, *"Nobody is stopping me. It's finally happening."*

## Conflict

Little did I know that my plan was going to be derailed along the way. Looking back, I am grateful to have lived through the experience, but it profoundly changed the way that I view the world, positively influence other fighter pilots and peak performers, and think about the time that I spend with others. In a way, the story influenced my achievement that eventually led to better success.

But it was painful, and it took me a really long time to talk about it.

# What are G-Forces?

G-forces are any acceleration due to gravity. It's the same type of feeling that you get when you are on a roller coaster and the chair bottoms out; it's the feeling of being squished into the seat.

## What is G-LOC?

G-induced loss of consciousness occurs when the human body experiences excessive and sustained G-forces that drain blood away from the brain causing cerebral hypoxia. In simpler terms, the human body is rendered unconscious because the blood and oxygen combination, that is crucial for normal functions, is taken away as the G-forces pull blood away from the cranium and towards the feet.

## What Is an Anti-G Straining Maneuver?

Pilots perform isometric muscle tensing combined with maintenance of adequate intrathoracic pressure by holding a preparatory breath followed by rapid air exchanges, in order to counteract G-forces encountered while flying. Tensing specific muscles and the use of quick air exchanges while under excessive G-forces, keeps blood and oxygen combinations at a level in the brain to remain alert in the high-G environment.

## Derailed

So to pick up where the story left off...I was taking an unwelcomed and violent fighter pilot nap and experiencing G-LOC for the first time.

The Big Mouth Block 30 F-16 fighter jet has flight controls that provide very rapid onset of G-forces. Coupled with the General Electric F110 engine and a lighter airframe, what remains is a G-force monster that will drive any fighter pilot to an unconscious state without the correct anti-G straining measures in place, physical conditioning, and hydration...don't forget the mindset.

My day started with a 55-mile bike ride and the usual tasks that accompany getting ready for a flight. Looking back, I don't remember anything going on in my life that would have caused me to think that I shouldn't be flying that day. I was mentally, physically, and spiritually ready to buckle up and get the job done.

What I didn't realize at the time was that one of the biggest factors physiologically for me was dehydration. The bike ride that I took in the morning wasn't something out of the norm, but it dehydrated me more than I knew. And by the time the hot afternoon rolled around, I had NOT consumed enough water for what I was about to do.

I wasn't ready, but I didn't know it.

On my sixth dogfight, all 6- to 9-G fights (6 to 9 times my body weight crushing down on me), I initiated aft stick pressure to command the maximum amount of turn performance I could, started my anti-G straining maneuver, got behind on my air exchanges, and without knowing it, LIGHTS OUT.

At 735 knots, 47 degrees nose low, quickly passing through 5,000 feet from the ground, I woke up.

Confused, disoriented, and mad, I initiated aft stick pressure again, got back on my anti-G straining maneuver, and recovered the aircraft.

*"Viper, knock-it-off."*

The fight was over, and we were going home. I lost physically and mentally. Even more crushing than knowing that I physically failed, my internal drive to "be the best" had been utterly crushed. I felt this all-consuming embarrassment like I'd never felt before in my life. I failed, and there was no hiding it.

Fortunately, the fighter squadron restarted my training only after a three-day course in a centrifuge where I painfully practiced my anti-G straining maneuver while under close supervision. I remember telling my flight commander, *"Don't give up on me because I'm not giving up."* You see, being a peak performer drives a character trait that can be confused by others as cocky, arrogant, and pushy. I hadn't yet learned everything I needed to from this situation, but my drive to succeed was all-consuming. And I wasn't about to give up!

## Transformation

The whole experience made me better, but it was painful. I was physically equipped to meet the demanding challenges of the high-G environment with additional training. This training made me physically and mentally stronger in the long run, and I'm fortunate to have lived to tell the story. Even more important, my internal transformation included some powerful thoughts that I carry forward with me through my personal and professional life that help me BE ready to tackle life's challenges.

---

### Slice's Wisdom:

Show up as ready as you can be. In the event you weren't ready, prepare your life to be ready for what may be next.

I have winning or learning experiences. I don't fail; I learn.

Temporary setbacks can be controlled with a positive attitude.

When broken, instead of running from the fear and pain of the situation, ask yourself what you can learn, and apply those ideas to your next challenge.

---

# JESSA "SMOKIN" CHARRON

"Smokin" is a wife, mom of 4, soon to be 5, and instructor pilot as a full-time reservist in the F-16 fighter jet. She believes that through stubbornness and tenacity that you can pursue any dream even when life gives you changes or setbacks.

*"Today you are you, that is truer than true. There is no one alive who is youer than you."*

**–Dr. Seuss**

# CHAPTER 19

# STUBBORN GRIT

G rit, perseverance, dedication, tenacity—these are all words that many people like to use for people who attain their goals.

I like to think that I am just stubborn. Maybe I was born that way. Maybe it's a family trait or part of my Catholic school upbringing. It is something that frustrates many people around me but yet has given me the ability to dig in my heels and generally get what I set out to get or accomplish. I have learned that I am an average and sometimes slightly above-average person when performing against my peers academically or in athletics. It took me a few years to accept that I wasn't extremely exceptional or one of a kind and be happy about it. I admit this in hopes you find something in my story that both inspires and motivates anyone who may feel like they aren't the cream of the crop but have big dreams.

I grew up in Nebraska with an older brother and two younger sisters. We were blessed enough to live on acreage, but with that came A LOT of chores. I also did competitive gymnastics.

By the time I was 12, we travelled to many different meets, and I competed as a level 10 (the highest level before qualifying for elite/Olympic level). I had practice every day for about three and a half hours, except Friday. On weekends or summer, the practice times usually were closer to 4-5 hours. My family all would work together to get the house cleaned and the lawn mowed, a six-hour process, on Sundays after church pretty much every week of my childhood.

If I had practice, I still had to get my share done before or after practice. My parents taught me how important hard work was from a young age, and I am so thankful even though sometimes that involved raking the gravel rocks after a rain storm created potholes and small canyons in the road. The only thing I knew I wanted when I was little was to be an Olympic gymnast and eventually be a mom. But not knowing exactly what I wanted to do when I grew up was ok. I just knew I wanted to make choices that set me up for options to succeed as long as I didn't quit and stayed stubborn.

Small victories each day just from chores and gymnastics taught me to be disciplined to get what needs to be done by setting priorities and doing what was in my power to have small wins through each day.

One day, my uncle, who used to be an F-15 pilot and was a United States Air Force Academy (USAFA) graduate, told me that women can't fly in combat. In my stubborn and "all-knowing" preteen way, I said *"Wanna bet?"* I never actually thought that I would fly or be a fighter pilot for that matter. It was my older brother's dream and my parents' vision for him.

My parents thought I'd be a doctor, but when they told me how many years of school it takes to be a doctor, I ruled that one out pretty quickly. (Little did I know, I would end up still doing plenty of extra school years anyway for my masters and education required for the Air Force/pilot training).

So, when it came time to decide where to go to college, I wasn't sure I could continue doing gymnastics for all four years since I would need a scholarship to not end up in a lot of debt after school. My brother was already at USAFA, and they had Division I gymnastics there. As a 17-year-old, I figured getting paid to go to school for a great education with no monetary debt and a guaranteed job sounded like a pretty good deal to me.

Plus, if I decided to quit gymnastics, then nothing would really change in my outcome (again making good choices to set myself up for success as long as I stayed stubborn). Turns out, I did compete all 4 years, and I am thankful my body was able to make it that far, since I struggled with a back injury from the age of 16.

When I started the Academy, I was only Navigator qualified due to my eyesight. I had surgery on my eyes when I was three since I was cross eyed. And no, even though I'm from Nebraska, I was not kicked by a mule, nor did I fall down a well. All jokes aside, I struggled passing the depth perception test. Somehow, I was able to get a "pilot spot" or assigned to Undergraduate Pilot Training (UPT) after graduating from USAFA.

However, just because I had the spot didn't mean I could go. I found out not only did I need a waiver for my eyesight but also that I am just a hair too short based on their requirements. So, rather than give up my pilot spot, I stubbornly insisted to pursue waivers for my "short" comings. My senior year of the Academy, I had to sit my stubborn self in different aircraft at a base in another state to try to pass the test to see if I could reach certain switches and brakes. I had to go to another separate location, this time all by myself to Brooks City Base in San Antonio, TX, to try to pass a "special" depth perception test. After some weird tests with my eyes dilated, I was able to pass with corrective lenses and was granted both waivers for height and eyesight.

Later on, I married my husband who was also going through pilot training. While we were busy, we made plans to stay together in our careers. We had two children shortly after pilot training while we were T-6 First Assignment Instructor Pilots (FAIPs), a gig we took to stay together longer with new babies, and then went through the F-16 basic course after that.

We were able to be assigned together at Misawa Air Base in Japan, and spent three and a half years there going to different deployments and Temporary Duty (TDYs) at opposite times. Luckily though, our kiddos only really remember the good times and barely remember the difficulty of juggling little kids and two full-time, active-duty fighter pilots. As a fighter pilot, we had long days that could be very stressful while we were in Misawa. Being stubborn still came in handy while we were so busy, making sure I was a fully prepared wingman and flight lead to go to combat while also making sure my two small children were cared for and loved. After Japan, we were assigned to Luke Air Force Base, Arizona, where we separated from active duty to join the 69th Fighter Squadron as reservists to continue flying fighter jets and pursuing our dreams. We had two more little girls, and we have another baby on the way.

Being a fighter pilot is hard work. I could have easily given up, or not even asked for what I believed was a dream job, even if I stole the dream from my brother. (But really, I just wanted to be like him.) I could have picked many other jobs, jobs that provide skills to transfer into the civilian world simpler than skills of a fighter pilot. I never thought I would want to stay in the Air Force as long as I have. But I would not quit.

Don't get me wrong; I have given up a few times in my life, but it is usually only momentary. I quit gymnastics when I was in eighth grade for a year because I felt like I was never going to be in the Olympics and I was missing out on "real" life. Turns out, gymnastics was my real life. Gymnastics was right for me. It kept me strong, disciplined, and thick-skinned. In the gym, it gave me confidence, like I could be more than just mediocre if I worked hard enough.

There are days when I am just "done" and don't clean up after myself or do the chores. But in the end, I know what has to be done, and my stubborn brain won't let me give up. I was generally not the best one in the class nor the very top, but I continued to work my hardest and finish to the best I knew how. No matter the goal, if you make the decision to do something, you can and will find a way to do it, no matter what. And hopefully, stubbornness (or as my mom says "stick-to-it-ive-ness"), luck and timing (or in my case, God) will help you along the way.

*Has anyone ever told you that don't measure up or can't do something because you lack a particular attribute or skill?*

*Do you ever feel like you don't fit in?*

---

### Smokin's Wisdom:

I work in a male-dominated community and throughout my career have faced many that think I don't belong. Yet thankfully, the majority of the people I have encountered have been really good supporters and friends.

Naysayers are everywhere and will demotivate you during your journey; be stubborn if you know where you want to go. And don't let anyone tell you otherwise. Even if you can't completely define your journey, do the work it takes to get there, and make the good choices along the way to clear your path.

*Wanna bet?*

---

# MELISSA "SHOCK" MAY

"Shock" is an American Patriot, retired fighter pilot, airline pilot, wife, mom and keynote speaker who loves to travel and experience living. Growing up as a "Granola" from Utah, she still loves the mountains for snowboarding, hiking and biking, but as of late, golfing is her new passion. Shock and her family are currently living in Costa Rica where she is learning to surf, hanging with monkeys and re-hacking the SCUBA certification. They call Colorado home.

> *"Make Voyages. Attempt them.*
> *There's nothing else."*

> **–Tennessee Williams**

Email Shock at maymelissa@hotmail.com.
Instagram: Shockf16 & Chickfighterpilots

# CHAPTER 20

# HANGING UP THE G-SUIT

Flying multimillion-dollar, high-performance fighter aircraft for twenty years was not the hardest thing I've ever done in my life.

The training to become a fighter pilot was not the hardest. It was not the six-month deployments away from home, in places that did not want us there. It was not jinking and maneuvering my jet while under hostile enemy fire. It was not squeezing into my G-suit, the inflatable "pants" designed to help prevent blood from pooling at our ankles when we pulled 9 times the force of gravity, or 9 Gs. It wasn't wearing my G-suit to keep me conscious yet still having all my blood capillaries break in my arms and legs while pulling 9 Gs. It wasn't the night I earned the Distinguished Flying Cross in Iraq.

Although extremely difficult to get through, the toughest thing I've done was not one of the several times there was an F-16 crash and we lost a pilot who was my friend from my base.

The opportunity to fly fighters was a gift. I took a leap of faith to go there. Being newly married to another officer, young, just starting our lives together, we had everything. We had our jobs. We had each other, and we had plans for our future. Our lives were mapped out: when we would start a family, when we would pay off debt, when we would own our home, when we would buy that motorhome and travel around the country. Going to pilot training, flying fighter aircraft, deploying, being geographically separated, adding a ten-year commitment to the military was never in our plans. The easy and comfortable road was to stay in our current situation. We would have lived happily ever after. Satisfied.

I risked it all. I risked my current job, my marriage, my happily ever after, and I went to Air Force Undergraduate Pilot Training. My attitude was, *"Work as hard as possible so there are no regrets at the end."* If I worked hard and got the airplane of my choice, it would all be worth it. If I worked hard and got an aircraft I didn't want, at least I wouldn't be left saying, *"I wish I had worked harder."* This has always been my motto. You cannot have regret if you give it your all, even if you don't get what you want. Fortunately, I got my first choice of F-16s.

I lived my happily ever after in a way I could never have dreamed! It turned out that my husband took the leap as well, and we both ended up flying F-16s together. I cannot imagine life in another way. Flying F-16s was the ultimate thrill, and it took me to amazing places, both geographically and mentally. The first night of Operation Iraqi Freedom, being one of the first manned flights into Baghdad, the world's most heavily defended city, I knew we would encounter hostile fire. I knew there was risk. I knew how to defend myself in my aircraft. What I didn't know is that would be the first time I knew I was okay with losing my life for my country if I needed to. We never think it will happen to us, but that night, I knew the risk was high. It was a gut check, and it required a mental toughness I did not realize I had within. One of my Air Force Academy classmates did pay the ultimate sacrifice that night.

My flying career was amazing. Handling a multi-million-dollar weapons system as the solo operator was a thrill that only a few have experienced. It's indescribable. The camaraderie shared among my fellow fighter pilots has given me lifelong friendships that most people outside of the military cannot understand. When you literally trust people with your life, the long-lasting bond that was formed will never be broken.

Because I took the risk of my career change to become a fighter pilot, I was able to live overseas for almost 10 years in Korea, Japan and Italy, and I was fortunate to have the opportunity to travel with the Air Force to several countries, including Singapore, Germany, Saudi Arabia, Poland, Bulgaria, the Netherlands, Spain, Portugal, Ecuador, Canada, Turkey and more. I traveled to places I never dreamed of going and doing things you only see on TV; it almost made my newlywed plans for a motorhome laughable. It was hard though. I'm not going to lie. There were long days and long deployments. There were broken jets and bad weather. There were good days and bad days, just like everything else. But I loved it. All of it.

## Shock's Wisdom:

After all of this, what was the hardest thing I've ever done?

The hardest thing I've ever done was to hang up my G-suit forever. It wasn't the training, the deployments, the enemy fire, the long days or the 9 Gs. The hardest thing I've ever done was deciding to retire from my life as a fighter pilot after 20 amazing years.

But I cannot imagine my life if I had never put the G-suit on. Thankfully, having the courage to take a leap of faith, change my career, risk the status quo and try something new changed me forever and has shaped my entire life. I would not change a thing. Take the jump and try on the G-suit because before you know it, you'll have to hang it up.

PART 3

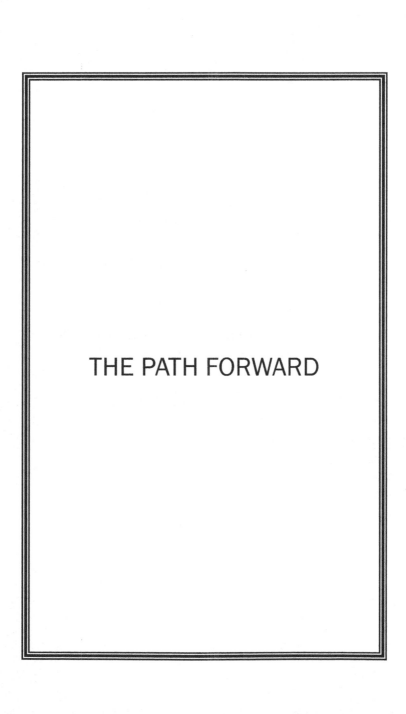

# THE PATH FORWARD

*"Eliminate the time between the idea and the act, and your dreams will become realities."*

**–Dr. Edward L. Kramer**

# CHAPTER 21

# HOW WE <u>GUIDE</u> PEAK PERFORMERS TO BECOME EVEN MORE SUCCESSFUL

What started as only an idea is now a reality. Sometimes ideas can upend your life and give you big challenges. Like this book that you are holding in your hand. It isn't easy convincing peak performing fighter pilots to do work, give money to charity, and use their time to help others; but they did and you get to reap the benefits now.

*Isn't it funny how that works?*

Listen, what I've been able to do is nothing special when you consider the facts. The facts are I've spent the last 20+ years of my life using trial and error methods to discover the secrets that I can GIVE you today for a small investment of time and energy.

I do not have superior intelligence. I wasn't blessed with excessive skill, nor did I have any other advantages going in, other than the ability to work hard, reframe my failures often, and never give up.

You can do the same thing I did. You can go out there and spend countless hours... dealing with all the stress, headaches and making all the same mistakes I did.

*My question is why?*

*Why would you do that when you can shave hundreds if not thousands of hours of headache and heartache off by simply exchanging a small amount of time for a proven flight plan to immediate success?*

Breeze past pitfalls as we give you the cumulative equivalent of millions of hours of unique experiences so that you can learn valuable shortcuts to achieve goals in a matter of hours or days instead of months or years.

When you look at it like that, I think you'll agree with me that you're getting the deal of the century when you join our life-changing community at:

**SingleSeatMindset.com/insider-circle**

# CHAPTER 22

# THE NEXT STEP

Information alone is not enough, but you already knew that. I want you to think about your first day in school. It's the first class, and you're bright-eyed and bushy-tailed and ready to learn. Your teacher walks in, drops a textbook in your lap and says, "Read this. I'll be back at the end of the semester to give you your finals."

This happens with your next class and every class that follows.

If that were the case, you would not be reading this today because you'd still be struggling to figure it all out.

Information is powerful, but on its own, it's not enough.

**You need more than just information.**

- You need <u>tools</u>.

- You need <u>community</u>.

- You need <u>accountability</u>.

You need an <u>elite group</u> of fighter pilots to guide you if you're going to make it happen.

Make the first step by joining our insider circle:

**SingleSeatMindset.com/insider-circle**

Then we'll immediately take you by the hand, and we'll walk the first steps together and then some.

*How much stress does failing to reach your ambitious goals cause in your mind and body right now?*

**Poof. It's gone.**

*Can you feel the difference just thinking about it now?*

Well, let's make it happen for real.

Get the afterburner results you deserve at:

**SingleSeatMindset.com/insider-circle**

# WHAT OTHERS ARE SAYING:

*"The wisdom contained in Single Seat Mindset gives you the tools to take your passion to the next level. It provides clear examples of transforming an average mindset into a high-performance attitude."*

**—Ethan Dunlap**

*"The Single Seat Mindset Insider's Circle provides short, meaningful and relevant lessons to keep your nugget in the game!"*

**—Young Wu**

*"Slice made mistakes, owned up to them, and shares lessons learned so that we don't have to repeat them. Single Seat Mindset has made me a better wingman and fighter pilot."*

**—Jacob Turner**

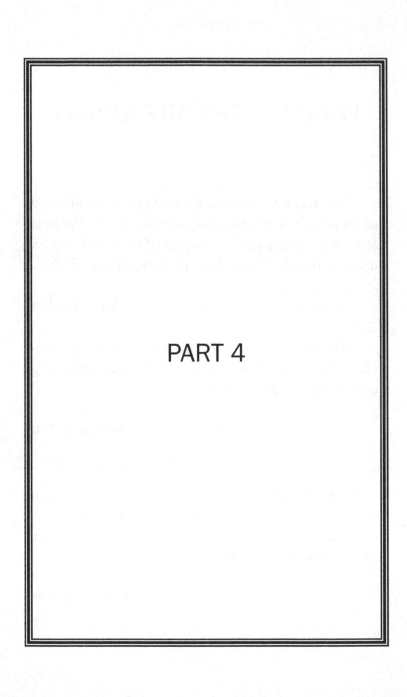

PART 4

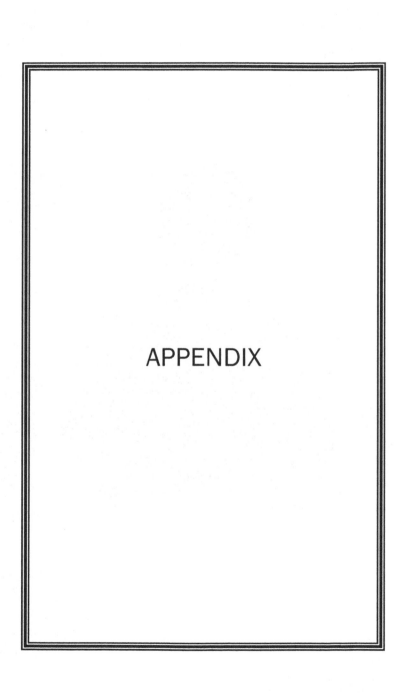

APPENDIX

Dominic "Slice" Teich

# ABOUT
# DOMINIC "SLICE" TEICH

Dom "Slice" Teich brings his fighter pilot background and applies them to guide pilots, athletes, business owners, and students with afterburner techniques that American fighter pilots use to ensure mission completion. As an Amazon best-selling author, business owner, entrepreneur, civilian and military instructor pilot, he knows that busy individuals and teams struggle with information overload.

Since 2002, "Slice" has guided hundreds of students toward their goals. His blueprint is called Single Seat Mindset; an impactful group of fighter pilot guides that combine their experience to lead driven individuals towards goal achievement. Proven formulas and life advice is shared to our insider circle community to ensure success and big goal achievement all while avoiding overwhelm, overload, and flame-out. They dive deep into the productivity world to provide guidance through short, actionable steps.

You won't find any other cutting-edge community like ours as we provide unique life experiences learned in the 3rd dimension.

### SingleSeatMindset.com

Access the Single Seat Mindset Insider Circle now at:

### SingleSeatMindset.com/insider-circle

# LOOKING FOR A UNIQUE INTERVIEW GUEST?

*"Dom is an excellent guest to have on your show. His knowledge of airplanes, leadership and mindset is excellent."*

**—Chris Shelor**
**Shelor Select Podcast**

*"Dominic is a fantastic guest.  He was interactive, funny and truly a good person to have on."*

**—Victoria Cuore**
**A Contagious Smile Podcast**

See if Slice is a good fit for your podcast or radio audience in less than 1 minute & 40 seconds. Please visit:

**SingleSeatMindset.com/podcast-guest**

# ABOUT
# SINGLE SEAT MINDSET

This impactful community of fighter pilot guides joined forces to help those that are ambitious and sick of others getting in their way as they blaze a trail towards success.

If you are a fast-paced, passionate, and highly competitive individual that wants to challenge the status quo, experience personal growth, and achieve success, join us today to access several hundred years of fighter pilot wisdom to generate afterburner results in your life at:

**SingleSeatMindset.com/insider-circle**

## How Single Seat Mindset Works

⇒ We give all profits to charity.

⇒ We guide peak performers with fighter pilot mindset.

⇒ Supported and authored by fighter pilots.

⇒ We provide a different perspective that can be applied to many different paths.

⇒ Use all the resources even if you aren't a fighter pilot.

⇒ If you are an aspiring pilot, you have come to the right place!

⇒ We want to sell you books in bulk, so please ask!

⇒ We will not give away your personal information.

⇒ We will ship all over the world as long as you coordinate with us.

⇒ We welcome feedback and opinions.

Bookstores, retailers, groups, schools, and other organizations: Please refer to our website for bulk discounts.

**SingleSeatMindset.com/books**

Thank you for being a part of this impactful community!

# PLEASE SHARE THIS BOOK

We would be grateful if you would share this book with your family, friends and various circles of influence, including:

- Schools and teachers.
- Coaches and sports teams.
- Family, friends and social networks.
- Personal groups.
- Church or parish groups.
- Business associates.
- Bookstores and libraries.
- Anyone trying to BE a bigger version of themselves.

For reduced pricing and bulk orders, we will send you dozens, hundreds, or even thousands of copies—with FREE shipping! Use our website to reach out to me so that I can coordinate your request with ease.

**SingleSeatMindset.com/contact**

# A SMALL REQUEST

Thank you for being a part of our life-changing community, Single Seat Mindset. Part of our powerful strategy is to keep giving back. It's a great return on investment to help others and to see others you empowered helping people too!

This offer isn't for the hobbyist or the person who won't take the shot because they are fearful that they might miss.

This is for serious individuals who won't let anything get in the way of their drive to reach their goals. Yes, what I'm offering will take less than one minute but in return gives others a lot more. *And isn't that what's most important? Giving back?*

If this book has provided a useful service to you or anyone else, we'd like to show off your comments and inputs!

Reviews are the BEST way to help us and others push through pain, hardship, and confusion so we all can BE better.

Please visit the following website to provide honest feedback so that you can help others achieve the biggest wins in the skies and on roads less traveled.

**SingleSeatWisdom.com/review**

If you have any questions or would like to tell me what you think about any of my books or services, please shoot me a message here:

**SingleSeatMindset.com/contact**

# WANT TO GIVE BACK?

1 00% of the proceeds support the Anna Schindler Foundation - a childhood cancer non-profit.

If you'd like to provide a direct impact to families that have children diagnosed with cancer, please make an impact today by visiting:

**AnnaSchindlerFoundation.org/donate**

If you are a fighter pilot and would like to be a part of the next volume of Single Seat Wisdom or contribute to others that want to follow in your footsteps, please contact me directly at:

**SingleSeatMindset.com/contact**

# Who Else Wants to Be a Published Book Author?

When it comes to flying his F-16, Dom Teich relies on a team of professionals to ensure his mission and safe flight are achieved. It's this team of behind-the-scenes men and women who allow Dom to do what he does best when it comes to flying.

When it comes to authoring a book, like the one you are reading at this very moment, Dom relies on the professionals at Bite Sized Books to ensure his books are the best they can be. To date, we have helped him publish four books in his "Single Seat" series with the unlimited potential of even more future books!

Bite Sized Books works with business owners, executives, consultants and coaches who want to leverage the power and profitability of being the author of a short, helpful nonfiction book. Our typical book is 100 pages long, which makes it much easier for readers to read and much faster for you to write!

Grab a FREE copy of the Amazon #1 Best Seller, *The 100-Page Book,* today and discover a smarter, more effective way to position you and your business.

Visit:

## 100PageBook.com

## **Business Is for Making Money—**
## *The 100-Page Book* **Will Make You Money!**

"Hiring Mike to assist with your book or marketing is akin to hiring a celebrity to attend a fund raiser for a charitable organization; it may cost more than you want, but the benefits will be 10X or higher shortly after you launch or implement his strategies and techniques garnered from 25+ years in the marketing industry. The upfront cost is well worth it as the backend payments will ripple through all aspects of your business. Don't waste another day banging your nugget against the wall trying to figure out what to do. Stop 'figuring.' Hire Mike and WIN HARD."

### **— Dominic "Slice" Teich**

**EVEN PEAK-PERFORMERS HAVE A BAD DAY.**

But there is one who never fails, one who passed
every test and even conquered death itself.
And he invites you to share in his victory.

Suffering produces perseverance, perseverance
character, and character hope.

FOLLOW THE
**ENDURING HOPE**
PODCAST
*with American Idol's*
**Scott MacIntyre**

scottmacintyre.com/podcast

OPEN YOUR HEART AND

## Give a hand to a child.

## OUR MISSION

The mission of the Anna Schindler Foundation is to support every family battling childhood cancer in the Inland Northwest and raise awareness of this disease. Since the beginning of the foundation, **we have helped over 400 families, giving over one million dollars in support to diagnosed families.**

## ANNA'S HOMES

The Anna Schindler Foundation has built townhomes in Spokane, Washington, for childhood cancer families from outlying areas who need to stay near Sacred Heart Children's Hospital.

To donate or for more information please visit:
**AnnaSchindlerFoundation.org**

198

# Helping Stellar Young Americans Chase Aviation Dreams

The mission of Cajun's Aviation Dream Foundation is to carry on the legacy of Major Stephen "Cajun" Del Bagno and introduce, foster, and build aviation dreams into reality for young minds eager to fly and pursue their passion for aviation.

## CajunsAviationDream.org

# HOW IT WORKS:

**We buy.**
**You invest.**
**We collect rent.**
**You get paid.**

View the FREE guide that answers the Top 20 most frequently asked questions about passive apartment investing.

ViperVenturesLLC.com

# HOW DO YOU REPROGRAM YOUR BRAIN TO TAKE ACTION ON COMMAND WITHOUT NEEDING SUPERHUMAN WILLPOWER OR DISCIPLINE?

Goal oriented individuals try everything when it comes to success...

... from a belief that they can do it alone to aggressive tactics that ruin the relationships that might help them get them to the finish line...

*"Why does being a goal-oriented individual have to be so DIFFICULT?"*

**Well, it doesn't have to be.**

It only takes a decisive mindset, a guide, and the CORRECT action to achieve success.

One little tweak in your gameplan every day is all it takes!

If you are stuck... restricted... frustrated... consider this your jet fuel that vectors your life on the correct trajectory in short, impactful steps, to avoid failure and achieve the success you deserve.

Follow the link below to join an insider-circle of fighter pilot knowledge and I'll reveal to you these life changing strategies when we launch so you can bypass the unnecessary rigidity of life that is slowing you down!

Get on the Single Seat Podcast list today:

**SingleSeatMindset.com/podcast**

# HIGH-IMPACT RESOURCES FOR PEAK PERFORMERS

The Single Seat Mindset Insider Circle is designed specifically for peak performers that desire cutting-edge ideas from some of the world's most elite fighter pilots. I would like to extend a personal invitation for you to be a part of our powerful community.

You can get direct access to all of our life changing resources... most of which are no cost to you! Additionally, you can contact me directly to ask your questions that deserve a unique perspective unlike anything found anywhere else in the world— a fighter pilot's perspective.

If you are a peak performer with a "Let's get it done; don't hold me back" attitude and want immediate results, get access now at:

**SingleSeatMindset.com/insider-circle**

Put your talents to good use, and accelerate past all the slow people holding you back from your ambitious goals.

Made in the USA
Las Vegas, NV
11 November 2023